D1003102

Chiara Corbella Petrillo

Simone Troisi and Cristiana Paccini

Chiara Corbella Petrillo
A Witness to Joy

Translation by Charlotte J. Fasi

SOPHIA INSTITUTE PRESS
Manchester, New Hampshire

Copyright © 2015 by Edizioni Porziuncola;
English translation Copyright © 2015 by Charlotte J. Fasi

Chiara Corbella Petrillo: A Witness to Joy is an English translation of *Siamo Nati e Non Moriremo Mai Più: Storia de Chiara Corbella Petrillo*, published in 2013 by Edizioni Porziuncola, Via Protomartiri Francescani, 2 –06088 S. Maria degli Angeli (Pg) – Italia (ISBN 978-88-270-1015-0).

Printed in the United States of America. All rights reserved.

Cover design by Coronation Media in
collaboration with Perceptions Design Studio.

Photos courtesy of Chiara's family and Edizioni
Porziuncola. Used with permission.

Biblical references in this book are taken from the Catholic Edition of the Revised Standard Version of the Bible, copyright 1965, 1966 by the Division of Christian Education of the National Council of the Churches of Christ in the United States of America. Used by permission. All rights reserved.

No part of this book may be reproduced, stored in a retrieval system, or transmitted in any form, or by any means, electronic, mechanical, photocopying, or otherwise, without the prior written permission of the publisher, except by a reviewer, who may quote brief passages in a review.

Sophia Institute Press
Box 5284, Manchester, NH 03108
1-800-888-9344

www.SophiaInstitute.com

Sophia Institute Press® is a registered trademark of Sophia Institute.

Library of Congress Cataloging-in-Publication Data

Troisi, Simone.
[Siamo nati e non moriremo mai più. English]
Chiara Corbella Petrillo : a witness to joy / Simone Troisi and Cristiana Paccini ; translated by Charlotte J Fasi.
pages cm
Includes bibliographical references.
ISBN 978-1-62282-305-5 (pbk. : alk. paper)
1. Corbella Petrillo, Chiara, 1984-2012. 2. Catholics—Italy—Biography.
3. Cancer—Patients—Italy—Biography. I. Title.
BX4705.C68145T7613 2015
282.092—dc23
[B]

2015025050

To Reverend Joseph F. Flanagan,
our "Father Vito,"
pastor of St. Gertrude Church,
Windsor, Connecticut,
1956-1976,
in appreciation

C.J.F.

We are born into eternity, and we shall never die.

Contents

Foreword

What We Have Seen

Much has been written of the things that we have witnessed . . .
These are the words that begin the Gospel of St. Luke. With
these same words Simone and Cristiana wished to begin their
biography of Chiara Corbella Petrillo.

The desire to know Chiara was immediately very strong, and
at her funeral, when I said at the end of my homily, "If you wish
to know more about Chiara, come ask us," people responded in
the thousands, urging us throughout the year to release testimonies, interviews, and material about her.

Thus, we instantly became aware of the high demand to hear
her story, a story that stuns and alarms and at the same time
charms. Many had already narrated the events of her story. There
were articles in the national dailies, complete chapters in books,
and discussions in blogs and in social media.

Moreover, as often happens in these cases, the (legitimate)
desire to understand combined with the scarcity of information
made way for interpretations and added details that had nothing
to do with the reality of the facts.

In consideration of all this and of the impossibility on the
part of her husband, Enrico, to cope with all the requests that
came from all over, the idea for this book was born. It became

the instrument to tell their story as it really happened. After overcoming the first natural resistance, owing to the fact that we had to share Chiara's story with masses of believers and non-believers, Enrico and I thought of asking Simone and Cristiana to write it. Always going back to St. Luke, we asked them to go over the whole story from the beginning and write an ordered account (cf. Luke 1:3).

This book reflects not simply the authors' points of view on what happened but also the accuracy with which Simone gathered the memories of relatives and friends. Those who witnessed, close up, all the events of Chiara's story make this book a testimony of faith by a portion of the Church that speaks of eternal life and actualizes the words of St. John, who writes in his Gospel: "[W]e speak of what we know, and bear witness to what we have seen" (John 3:11).

— Father Vito D'Amato

Preface

In Order Not to Forget

I am here now, in your room, your last room. You slept here only one night, and now it is your room. It is here that the doors were opened and He came in person to meet you. It is the room where your loving eyes finally recovered. In brief, I am here in this holy place, and I am reminiscing.

Only a year has passed since that last, unique Mass was cele-brated in this room. I am moved by all the love that was received and given here, always together, and I discover again how much in love I am with you and with Him.

Perhaps, however, it is still too easy for me. I have been nurtured too well. I have eaten the "honey from the rock" [Ps. 81:16], to cite a biblical reference. The ... best [pasta] carbonara, I would say. Again, it is here that He told us in the Gospel of that last Mass, "You are the salt of the earth ... the light of the world" (Matt. 5:13–14). It was and it is His mandate to "go out and proclaim [that] the kingdom of heaven is close at hand" (cf. Matt. 10:7).

There is a world [out there] that loves you in an extraordinary way. It feels close to you in its sufferings. It prays to you as if you were already a recognized saint. I would like to tone it down a bit, although I have no doubt that you truly are. Your happiness almost seems the imprimatur of the Lord: as if to say, "Here I passed; this is my space."

You know, my love, our love continues to generate children (Father Vito made me aware of it). We have so many that I cannot remember all their names. They are children not in the flesh; rather, they are children in the Lord.

I hope that Francesco will forgive me, but I opened his gift, your letter to him for his birthday. I wrote some of it myself, and I think I should share it with the children far away. I hope I did not err. I did not think that I was depriving Frankie of your love, for he is the child of your flesh.

You know, there are also those in the world who would prefer that you never existed, because it is not easy to be judged by God in you: in your eyes, in your bandage, in your smile. In you, in the totality of your beauty, there is always He. Therefore, this book is necessary. My love, there is already a book about you; we are still marveling over it! It is not a book that explains the truth. The truth knows very well how to explain itself. Nor does the book exist to generate publicity (as many would have wished). There is never complete truth in anyone who wishes to sell you something. But you, yes, you can say it because you have given all that you were able: life.

It was necessary for you to die, my love; it was necessary—so that the blind see, so that the thirsty drink, so that the arrogant are routed in their heart, and so that His people know that slavery has ended and that the King comes in glory.

This book exists simply to give witness to the one who wishes to open his heart to the reality that God is good and that one can die happy. Above all, it helps me not to forget. I have seen, only through grace, what many prophets and kings would have wished to see but did not [cf. Luke 10:24]. I would be culpable if I were silent. I must testify—I from here, and you from there, united in love that, for us, is different but certainly not weaker.

I thought of Simone and Cristiana to write this book. Who better than they, the intimate friends with whom we shared so many secrets of our souls walking together in the same direction, speaking the same language? They also witnessed this marvelous story. I thought of them, and I am sure that I did the right thing. I would have liked to have written it myself, but in a rare moment of infinite honesty, I said to myself: "But when? I still do not understand which drawers contain the socks and which the underwear!" Better they. They seem perfect. I shared this idea with Father Vito, and he blessed it.

Then I informed them. And they prayed. They are of pure hearts, and they desire what is good. They were always there, from when we knew them at Assisi as engaged couples. We were at their wedding, and they were at ours, a month later. They were there to pray outside the door when Maria was born and then at her funeral. They were there when Davide was born and again at his funeral. They were always there, at the birth of Francesco and finally at our Passover, when everything was completed. Who better than they to write this book?

Simone has a background in journalism and publishing. He has all the necessary qualifications to spread your story effectively. Cristiana is the friend with whom, more than all the others, you shared the Faith. She knows some of the secrets of your heart ... conversations between women of superior intelligence. How beautiful the ways of Providence.

And so they did it. It was difficult for them. They prayed together every morning before they began to work. They listened to hours and hours of testimony gathered from the closest friends. They assembled and transcribed everything with care, and they finished writing not a romantic book but a book that speaks of you, of us, and especially of God, of how He loves. It is only the first book. I know that there will be many others in many languages.

You have spoken much to me with heavy words that seemed to come from theological tomes. Who knows if, when you said them, you were aware of it? I am quite sure that you were.

I diligently pointed them out in order not to forget them. Yes, of course, in order not to forget.

—Enrico Petrillo

Chiara Corbella Petrillo

Introduction

A Close Friendship

"My name is Chiara. I am twenty-five, and I have been married to Enrico for a year and a few months. This evening, if I can do it, I shall tell the story of our daughter, Maria Grazia Letizia, who was born June 10 of this year."

It was November 19. Chiara gave this testimony in the Church of Saint Frances of Rome (Santa Francesca Romano) at Ardeatino, in Rome. Her words that evening touched many hearts. It is an inspirational story, and she told it simply and with the sincerest spontaneity. There was no way of misunderstanding it, just as, Chiara said, no one can misunderstand the truth that "God places in each one us."

Chiara and Enrico had decided to go forward with the pregnancy of the anencephalic baby girl, and so she was born, she was baptized, and then just half an hour later she was taken to the Heavenly Father. Now, five months after the funeral, during which Chiara played the violin and Enrico played the guitar and sang his songs, they were there relating the mysterious joy that had accompanied them on this journey.

Just three years later, many of those who came to know Chiara through that testimony would attend her funeral in the same church. And it was truly something special to feel oneself a part of it. On that occasion, Father Vito, the Petrillos' spiritual director, invited everyone to consider how this family, in the interval, had accepted another baby, a boy, who also died after birth. And then they bore with trust and peace the illness that Chiara lived during her third pregnancy.

Anyone who wished to know more of Chiara and Enrico's story would have found, among their relatives and friends — witnesses of this extraordinary life — a willingness to speak of how things had gone. And so here we are. We are among the witnesses. Incredibly, we found ourselves next to Chiara and Enrico at every step.

This book exists thanks to the questions of those who grew close to Chiara, even if only after hearing of her story. Through God's gift to us, we have lived this journey of grace with them: all the marvels, from the downpours, of which there were many, to the beautiful rainbows after a powerful storm.

* * *

Who is Chiara? Why is there so much attention surrounding her? What has she done? At first sight, this is the dramatic story of a mother who died of a tumor, leaving her son and her husband alone. Perhaps it is a story similar to many others. But something here does not square. Everything in this story was lived in joy, and it became life for many others.

Like a little child who follows the aroma of a cake as it is taken from the oven, many have followed the "perfume of sanctity" of these two newlyweds who recognized in their suffering their dance; who, smiling, confronted the hardest trials; and who together discovered the happiness to which each of us is called. Throughout, an inebriating perfume clings to you, even though initially you fearfully combat it.

A Close Friendship

Who or what brought Chiara to a death like this? We have listened to the One who loved her with a unique love, stronger than any storm. We have retained in our memory all those moments that the Lord has allowed us to share with her (and with Him), because this story contains a message. It is a credible and solid announcement of what happened two thousand years ago and what continues to occur each day since then. "[T]o all who received him ... he gave power to become children of God" (John 1:12).

A person dies as he lives. Chiara died in an amazing manner, smiling in the face of death. Much more than serene, she was happy. Being next to her was watching the living and the dying of a child of God.

There is a photo of Chiara and Enrico that shows them walking away, embracing each other. We took that photo on April 4, 2012, less than an hour after we heard the doctors' verdict. They were on one of the bridges that overlook the Tiber Island (Isola Tiberina) and the Fatebenefratelli, the Roman hospital that Chiara and Enrico left for the nth time, always the same way, embracing each other. Invariably, without knowing it, we had arrived at the hospital at the right moment.

While we were walking behind them, holding Francesco in the baby sling, at a certain point Chiara and Enrico turned around and, holding their hands like pistols, pretended to shoot at Francesco, saying, "Bum, bum" at each shot. Francesco laughed and waved joyfully. He was ten months old. We accompanied them to the car parked on the Lungotevere (the boulevard that runs along the Tiber River), and we embraced each other in tears. Chiara did not waste even that moment to demonstrate her love.

It was at Assisi that our simple and deep friendship began. We had already known each other, but in the shadow of Portiuncula we became brothers and sisters. It was beautiful to make life's journey together. We were married a few weeks apart, and from there our relationship never slackened. We spoke about everything: from the most ordinary, such as chicken à l'orange or what to plant in the garden, to the most meaningful, such as Paradise and death. We shared the everyday reality of newlyweds; we knew their first two babies and the joys and challenges of their parenthood. When the illness arrived, we saw close up how life conquers death. We spent entire days speaking, asking the important questions, hoping together. Like the alpinists, we walked *in cordata* (on the rope), each one ready to pull when the other tired.

We were spectators and protagonists of each happening in their story. Often with Chiara, we asked each other why. Perhaps we will discover why only when dying, when Love explains everything to us.

Next to them, there was no difficulty believing in eternal life. It seemed to touch Chiara. We were already aware of being immersed in it. One of the greatest gifts they demonstrated to us was that we have only today. And in this present you can be happier than you ever had the courage to imagine. It is in the ordinary things that the extraordinary acts of God can intervene. Chiara and Enrico learned in a marvelous way how to make space for grace; and grace cannot wait to show us the marvels of what it can do.

The deception is in thinking that this is a privileged experience reserved for Chiara and Enrico, as if they were special. But God is the Father of each one of us in the same way. Many times, looking at Chiara and Enrico, we thought that if this is how God helps, we also can bear our cross.

Their marriage was the foundation of everything. In this sacrament, grace was multiplied. On the [nuptial] altar, they were

A Close Friendship

transformed before our eyes. Little by little we watched them give back each thing: Maria Grazia Letizia, Davide Giovanni, little Francesco, their plans as a young couple, but above all, their love, the hardest part. We do not recall a day of desperation. Indeed, their joy increased. They recognized everything as a gift, and they were wise enough to understand that this earth is not our fatherland and that we are not at the point of arrival. At the same time, even our palate changed: "That which seemed bitter to me was changed into sweet in body and soul."[1]

The body is made for love; this is its objective. It is through the body that evil, frustration, and pain reach us all our days. But the good news is that precisely through another Body comes consolation and salvation. Chiara and Enrico have demonstrated this through their story; they have lived their marriage as a secure path to sanctity, as a complete vocation.

* * *

If *miracle* is understood as a physical recovery, then this book contains no miracles. There are no cures. The miracle we narrate is another. It is a disarming joy, simple and pure: a treasure to discover. It is the perfect joy of Francis of Assisi ("O mysterious joy," as Enrico would say) that changes evil into good, that opens your heart and your horizons.

To discover that you are loved is the center of all existence. And when we are filled with this total and delirious love, little by little, we grow and love in turn. That gradualness in our journeys is a sign of the infinite tenderness of God.

The Lord had also outlined a very special pedagogy for our friends, a path of maturation through love. Accompanying Maria

---

[1] *Fonti Francescane* (Padova: Editrici Francescane, 2004), 99, n. 110.

Grazia Letizia to her birth in heaven was only the first of the "small possible steps" of which Chiara spoke.

"Small possible steps," says Enrico, "is what our story is about. First we accompanied one child to eternity; then another; then, finally, we became pregnant with a beautiful, healthy child only to discover that Chiara had a tumor; then we discovered that we must wait."

Finally there were the treatments, the therapies. Yet, in spite of all this, their faces were always sunny, serene, and smiling; and always with an authentic smile. Seen from the outside, all these trials are frightening. We wondered if we could ever confront anything similar. But each step is accompanied by a necessary grace.

Chiara would become very angry when anyone attributed to her the special gifts of courage, all her own, that permitted her to confront all these challenges. She often told us that by nature she was timid. Smiling, she told us that at school she never went confidently to take oral exams, even when she had studied and felt prepared. She was always anxious.

She always responded that if she could do it, anyone could. Strength comes in making space, in trusting in God, in truly believing that God is good and that He has only astonishing things in mind for you.

"One's look," Pope St. John Paul II wrote, "expresses what is in the heart"; it is "a threshold of the interior truth."[2] Whoever has exchanged glances with Chiara knows that she does not lie—that there is really hope and that such hope is valid for

---

[2] St. John Paul II, general audience of September 10, 1980, cited in Yves Semen, *La spiritualità coniugale secondo Giovanni Paolo II* [*The Conjugal Spirituality of God according to John Paul II*] (Torino: Edizioni San Paolo, 2011), 67–68.

everyone. Also for this reason it was truly good to be part of the Petrillos' lives.

* * *

Chiara not only knew how to listen, but she held in high esteem the opinions and counsel of others. A particular trait that describes her was service. Not holding back in little things permitted her to express her gratitude also in things much greater. Chiara freely accepted her deprivations and her dependence. You are someone when you belong to someone, and knowing how to belong to Jesus permitted Chiara to be what she was. Depending on Him, she renounced understanding, choosing instead to express words of benediction to God and to whoever was next to her. Giving of herself was the only true possibility. And at a certain point, that is what Chiara chose to do. She truly embraced her cross, because "God is the highest good that gives value to everything that exists," and He is the "fullness of that joy that does not vanish, not even when it is bathed with tears."[3]

Perhaps Chiara's story is meant to show that the beauty of matrimony, with its urgencies, its gifts, and its struggles, is really a path that sanctifies. The married couple, indeed, reveals to the world how God loves.

"We do not at all feel courageous," Chiara related at one point, "because in reality the only thing that we have done is said yes, one step at a time." This statement has been a small treasure. It contains all that there is to know.

Prayer and fraternity were fundamental, because Chiara and Enrico said that without prayer, they would not have been able

---

[3] Anna Maria Canopi, "Credere, La gioia della fede," *La riflessione. Solo l'umile incontra Dio*, no. 3 (2013): 45.

to do anything and because so many, not only those closest to them, but many throughout the world, have prayed for them. They were joined, little by little, by new companions on this journey. Each one arrived at the right moment, each one a sign of Providence, each one sustaining them in the most difficult phases: they were that little flame that lit up the dark, each one adding his testimony to ours: the family, friends, and doctors who traveled all or part of this journey with them.

In these years we have seen how Chiara's story has been diffused in an unexpected manner. It entered into homes, into hospitals, and into so many other stories. To relate the effects of all this would require another entire book. Immediately after her death, interest in her began reaching up to the stars (in every sense), leaving us stunned and grateful.

"All this light," Enrico said, "is diffusing without my doing anything. Cardinal Vallini [the pope's vicar in Rome] called me and said that he would come to Chiara's funeral.... We have always marveled at all the love that has surrounded us."

* * *

In brief, why this book? Because so many wish to know Chiara, to understand how she managed to live and to die in the way that she did. Many know only that she was a young woman who died after postponing some cures until after the birth of her baby. But there is much more. Left behind is a beautiful marriage, lived in fullness and joy and with a love so true that it led both spouses to share the same cross. This, and all that we have witnessed, we shall relate to you.

Beauty will save the world, Dostoevsky wrote. Yes, but which beauty: the beauty of a face happy in suffering, the face of Jesus? This is the beauty that Chiara showed us.

1

"Perhaps I Did Not Understand"

The words of the holy one, the true one,
who has the key of David,
who opens and no one shall shut,
who shuts and no one opens.

—Revelation 3:7

To love a person means:
to accept not understanding
everything about her,
being prepared to be changed and to suffer,
to renounce something for her.

—From Chiara's notes

Chiara and Enrico met at Medjugorje in the summer of 2002. He was on pilgrimage with his prayer community, Charismatic Renewal, and she was on vacation in Croatia with some high school classmates. Seeing that her sister, Elisa, was also at Medjugorje, Chiara decided to join her.

Chiara was born in Rome on January 9, 1984. She and Elisa, two years older, had a very close relationship. They and their mother, Maria Anselma, belonged to a community called The

Heart of Jesus of the Renewal of the Spirit. They prayed from a very early age, at least fifteen minutes a day, as members of the Renewal.

Chiara was talented in drawing and in music (she studied first the piano and then the violin). There emerged in her a certain autonomy that rendered her very determined in her choices, but she was not rebellious. Rather, she possessed a tranquil dignity that she expressed in service to others. Both Maria Anselma and Elisa remember how, as a baby, Chiara, who, as the smallest, would be the first person served at the table, would take her full plate and pass it to Elisa, so that her sister could eat before her.

Thanks to her father's work, which earned him commissions on behalf of the tourist industry, the family was able to travel a great deal. They were pleasant times. Chiara's vacation in Croatia with friends was supposed to have been one like many others. "But there was an unforeseen encounter," Chiara would say later. "I wished to make a pilgrimage; I did not expect to return home with a boyfriend."

Enrico did not foresee it either. He was on that pilgrimage with his girlfriend. But something went wrong, and they broke up precisely while on that trip.

During a meal in the hotel, Enrico raised his eyes and saw Chiara coming toward him, toward the only seat available. Her beauty immediately impressed him. He felt that it would take little to fall in love with her. Chiara, looking at Enrico and imagining that he was not alone, immediately thought: "Oh! This boy is mine"—in the sense of "he is for me," Enrico clarified later. "It was an intuition, and each of us had the same thought at the same time. It was a long road at the beginning—we gave each other the first kiss after five months. She had said no to so many suitors. She was waiting; she knew that the right one for her would come along." In fact Chiara had never dated anyone steadily before then. Enrico was twenty-three, and Chiara was eighteen. The day was August 2.

* * *

After they returned to Rome, they got to know each other and decided to go together. In certain ways, it was an ordinary relationship, like many others, punctured by arguments, breakups, and reconciliations.

Married couples are capable of giving themselves to each other only if they first learn to say everything, to bare their hearts, to let each other into their lives, and to confront problems together. It requires a commitment from the very beginning of a relationship, and it is not easy. Chiara was afraid of revealing herself for what she really was. She feared saying no would cause her to lose Enrico. [On his part,] Enrico was afraid of losing the people he loved. That fear had come upon him at the death of his father.

"From an early age, I always had a great fear of dying," Enrico related. "I lost my father to a heart attack when I was twenty-three. It was the most difficult death I had ever confronted, and it took me several years to recover. I had to learn to accept the fact that people you love might die at any time. This impeded me from loving her deeply."

The relationship did not go smoothly. There were painful breakups. The first occurred in 2006, after a particularly critical period in which they quarreled very often. "When we left each other," Chiara related, "I said, 'Okay, Lord, you made me meet him at Medjugorje, so you explain to me why you took him from me.'"

The possibility of missing the target, of losing, with Enrico, "her own vocation," was an enormous suffering, a true misery. Enrico missed Chiara, but it was also a fact that they were not able to stay together serenely.

Two days after the breakup, Chiara departed for Medjugorje on the first available ship. All the confusion and bitterness that had accompanied her during that trip seemed to have dissolved once she climbed Podbrdo (Apparition Hill), "the mountain of the apparitions."

"After I arrived on the mountain, I felt such peace, as if to say: 'Be serene.' I continued to tell myself: 'Yes, okay, be serene. What does that mean? What must I do? Do I go back to him? Must I call him, or should I not call him?' I continued to look inside myself for the resources that were no longer there: I had already played all my cards, and they had not worked. I continued to look for a human solution, and instead the Lord was telling me: 'Wait and trust.' "

When Chiara returned, she thought again of Enrico. She called him, but the conversation turned into another argument, and at the end of the phone call, she made a firm decision to forget him. At that time, she had the opportunity to travel to Australia with her father and her sister. "My thought was, 'In Australia I will be able to forget Enrico and put my soul at peace.' "

On her return from Australia, Chiara turned on the computer and read her e-mail messages. Enrico had not known anything about her trip; he saw her online on the Internet, and he sent her an e-mail. She had gone on vacation to forget him, and now here he was again, there in front of her.

He was asking her for the exercise weights that he had left at her house. So it was not an excuse [at least not a conscious excuse]. Enrico did not know what she was living through, and above all he did not know how much his fears were impeding him from being happy.

For Enrico, loving that girl was too difficult, and ceasing to do so unburdened him. Now he was okay, even serene, but when he saw her arrive with the box of his things, he was taken aback. He said to her: "I did not expect you to bring them yourself." As a matter of fact, it was not her style, and Enrico was stunned.

[But] Chiara's attitude was already changing; she was beginning to trust, as the Lord had told her to, and she had begun to wait. "Perhaps," Chiara remembered later, "the Lord was already training us for all that He would ask of us later."

From that meeting the two began to see each other again, and soon they were back together.

* * *

Chiara chose to go to Assisi on December 8 for a vocational course given by the Friars Minor of Portiuncula, and at the end of it, she asked Father Vito to become her spiritual director. On her return, Enrico found her changed. He decided to reassess his life; and a few weeks later, he went to Assisi for the New Year vocational course.

"I understood then that it was worth the pain to live only if one was disposed to love truly," said Enrico. "Then I decided to have Father Vito as my spiritual director and to begin a new journey." And that is how Father Vito also entered the life of Enrico.

After a few months, Enrico and Chiara's relationship encountered new jolts, and soon it did not hold up. In the spring of 2007 they separated again. "The last time we broke up, Enrico went to speak with Father Vito, and the next day I went. And Vito said to me: 'But why are you so stubborn?' I said to him: 'Vito, I do not know!'"

In this particular crisis, Chiara was drawn to recall the greatness associated with marriage. In losing Enrico, she felt she was losing the possibility of being happy, of being with the right person. She was right. But it was also true for her that there was a primary fundamental passage to complete. Chiara had to accept the possibility of having misunderstood. She had to experience first the love that the Lord had for her.

"Then Father Vito gave me this verse for my meditation: 'When God opens a door, no one closes it; when God closes it, no one opens it.' [cf. Rev. 3:7]. This phrase changed my life." That phrase also made Chiara a Christian.

Enrico was very firm on this point: "If you recognize that you can love only in God, you must love God more than your wife, more than your husband. If you look for consolation in the love of a person who is near you, you are taking the wrong path, because only the Lord can give you consolation; and then, if the Lord wishes, He gives you consolation through another person." Enrico turned back to God, precisely because it was God who had given him Chiara.

At the same time, their story was not succeeding at all. Chiara was not able to give back joy and life to her relationship. Still, as at the wedding at Cana, although she was not able to change water into wine, she was able to fill the jars with water (see John 2:1–12); she was able to obey that Word of Jesus and experience that He is the Living One. Letting herself be drawn by Him and opening the door to Him, she discovered that she was able to stop hiding herself, and finally without fear she showed herself.

"Perhaps I Did Not Understand"

The little verse from Revelation wished to say precisely this: "If he is your spouse, if he is for you and you are serene, no one will take him from you."

"At that moment I said: 'Okay, perhaps I did not understand anything.' Vito continued to ask me: 'Do you want him, do you want your Tobias [cf. Tob. 6–7]? Do you want the person the Lord has thought of for you? Do you believe that there is a man who has been thought of only for you?'

"I said: 'Yes, I believe it.'

"And Vito responded: 'Then let it be the Lord who leads you to him, okay?'

"At that moment I abandoned all my plans, such as: 'Now I shall do this.... Now I shall convince him in this way.... Now I shall do it my way,' and I felt truly liberated, and I said: 'Perhaps I did not understand anything; perhaps it is not Enrico ... Yet it seemed to me that it was Enrico.... Oh well, Lord, I do not understand anything!'

"After forty minutes of this conversation, I cried, and then I thought, 'Enough of this.' And to Vito passing me the tissues, I said: 'No, no, I am okay,' but I continued to cry."

Choosing marriage, like consecrating oneself to religious life, also requires a vocation. It is more than simply a natural inclination; it is necessary to respond to a special call from God. But to what does God call us? What does He ask us to do? Marriage can make saints. But it is necessary for spouses to love each other as Jesus loves the Church.

The logic is that of the cross: giving oneself first without asking anything of the beloved, leading to the goal of the radical gift of oneself. Love is demanding. Marriage is demanding. If one does not respond to this request, then one is not looking on marriage as a vocation, but simply as accompanying one another to death.

Indeed, conjugal spirituality is an authentic vocation in itself and not a "Series B." Spouses are called to a true sanctity on which the realization and happiness of a person depends. But this road must be taken up before marriage, during the "furnace" of courtship and engagement.

If there were need to demonstrate it, it would be enough to cite Chiara's saying that the difficulty of courtship was the hardest trial that she had lived. And she repeated it many times. Also during the last days of her life, when she spoke of herself, she dedicated the majority of her time and her words to this phase. Not even the first two pregnancies or her illness were greater than the pain she felt thinking that her life would not be tied to Enrico's. Without that trial, everything would have been different. Going through it permitted her and her husband to do all that they did. "If you feel loved," Enrico said, "you can do everything. If you have felt his love, you can also enter into the fire. I can do everything because love did not disappoint me. Indeed, it surprised us."

After some time, Chiara finally experienced her turning point. Enrico called to speak with her and also to vent his frustration about their relationship, which seemed unable to go forward. During that encounter, for the first time, Chiara cried. And she could not stop.

"On that occasion, the thing that truly struck Enrico was that he saw me for what I was. Even at that moment, I still tried to be better than I was; up to that point, I had always tried to be better than I thought of being. I forced myself to be better. But in that moment, Enrico really saw how I was made: he saw that I no longer had the desire to create pretenses in order to make our story good at all costs. I was before him without defenses, and I thought only: 'Let us see what happens.'"

"Perhaps I Did Not Understand"

Chiara passed from thinking that she had a right to Enrico to the understanding that the other is a gift of God. Therefore, it was necessary first to accept losing him in order to find him. Father Vito relates: "Chiara understood precisely during the engagement that if that was not her mission, if Enrico were not the person that God had thought of for her, then he must let her go for the good of both of them." It was a teaching that would be useful to her in each of her small possible steps.

Seeing her like this, Enrico proposed to Chiara that they go on vacation together. He thought of it as a last attempt to make their relationship work.

He thought of *something* he could do. Chiara thought instead of *someone*. She thought of an encounter with a person who might get involved in their story and lend support. She thought of the Franciscan March, one of the initiatives of the Brothers Minor of Assisi. It is a ten-day hike on foot to Portiuncula, with the arrival scheduled on the feast of the Pardon of Assisi.[4] It is one of the most popular ventures, and little time remained to make a reservation. Enrico said that he would agree to go only if they succeeded in reserving a place immediately. Chiara succeeded on the first attempt. Responding on the other end of the telephone line was Father Vito: "You made it! Good! They are the last two places."

---

[4] The Pardon of Assisi refers to the plenary indulgence that St. Francis obtained from Pope Honorious III in 1216 after having a vision while praying in the church of the Portiuncula. The indulgence is granted to the faithful who visit the Portiuncula (or any parish or Franciscan church) on August 2 and fulfill the usual conditions for obtaining an indulgence: sacramental Communion and confession within eight days and prayers for the Holy Father.

* * *

They departed at the end of July. It was a march of twenty kilometers a day, tiring but beautiful. All the young people who participate each year share in the desire to recover all that is good, authentic, and beautiful hidden in their stories. For Enrico and Chiara, aching but happy, it was a journey to heal their hearts. Along the road on such a journey, all defenses fall away—first the physical, then the mental. The backpack [a symbol of both] forces the hiker to abandon the superfluous, everything that impedes him from going forward.

Enrico and Chiara had so many things to abandon. During the march, Father Vito was next to them. He told them to pray so that the Lord could heal the wounds that they had caused each other. The prayer was heard.

"On the sixth day of the walk, Enrico and I found ourselves walking together," Chiara related. "He looked at me and said: 'Shall we get married?' I looked at him and said: "Yes, Enri.... Okay." And I was thinking: 'But we broke up a week before this trip!'

"But he insisted: 'No, no. I am serious: shall we get married?' And I: 'Enri! Yes.... Okay.' And I was thinking: 'This guy has sunstroke.'"

But Enrico was not joking. He distanced himself a little from the road and, picking a sunflower from the nearby field, approached her.

"I am serious. Let's get married."

Chiara looked at him. "I responded: 'Okay.' And I thought: 'Who knows if he'll remember this tomorrow morning.'" She began to tease, "I hope you remember!"

Enrico and Chiara had come to an agreement. They had argued and broken up more than once. At a certain point, however, they grew weary and decided to do things seriously. And they both arrived at the desire to say yes.

To change everything meant to take a different view of things, to adapt a phrase that was both old and new: "The only extraordinary thing is to be children of God. We must only choose: we can believe in a Father who loves us, or we can continue to think that life is a gamble."

Wounded by life, by his relationship with Chiara even up to that moment, Enrico had faulted her for all that was ugly in his life. This, he had thought, gave him a right to mistreat her, to revenge himself on her. "Chiara," recalls Father Vito, "was his San Damiano crucifix, before which a young Francis became aware that the true victim is someone else. It is the person before him, who loves him, even while he is angrily throwing daggers at him."

"We who think we are victims in life," Father Vito said, "change solely before Him, before this love [Fr. Vito is explaining St. Francis's conversion before the crucifix of San Damiano at Portiuncula]. To transform everything is to see Someone who is dying for you while you are killing Him. To transform everything is to see a Son of God who shows clearly that you either give life or you take it—that if you do not love, you kill."

And the first thing that happens is that the desire to become a child of God bursts upon you. It is the gift granted by the Father to each one who accepts the Son into his life in all the ways the Son wishes to present Himself.

The last months before their marriage "went as smooth as oil," Chiara said.

* * *

It was precisely during those months of preparation for their wedding, in the spring of 2008, that we (Simone and Cristiana) encountered Enrico and Chiara at Portiuncula. We had just moved to Assisi.

Immediately there was an awesome connection between us. We spoke endlessly of faith and Providence, of our experiences and the journey that, up to that moment, had led us there. Chiara and Enrico asked us how we felt leaving our parents and transferring so far from Rome. They told us that they wanted to get married and were waiting for Chiara to graduate.

But then, during that Paschal Triduum of 2008—while participating in the adoration of the Cross on Good Friday—everything became clear. They understood that there was no time to lose. It was time to fix a date.

That evening we said goodnight to each other with the promise to keep in touch. And if it served, we would help them plan their wedding.

What really impressed Simone and me was the incredible trust between us and Enrico and Chiara. It was as if we had found a couple with whom we could really share our life, something that rarely occurs and only with certain very close friends.

We understood each other at once. The same things annoyed us, and we were attracted by the same opportunities. We all agreed that our happiness existed in matrimony and that we wished to live it seriously, as a vocation: everything or nothing. All of us had fears regarding financial responsibilities, especially housing and work. But we each plucked up our courage. Chiara was especially disposed to entrust herself to accept this "challenge."

In the following months we heard from each other and visited several times. In order to alert their parents of their plans to marry, Chiara borrowed our idea of inviting them out to dinner. It went very well.

"Perhaps I Did Not Understand"

At the end of May, we notified Enrico and Chiara that we would be married in a little more than two months, on August 15. They were surprised by our decision but Chiara wrote to Cristiana that our "craziness" encouraged them in their choices. They decided to marry on September 21.

2

Live and Let Yourself Be Loved

Whoever receives one such child in my name
receives me; and whoever receives me,
receives not me but him who sent me.

—Mark 9:37

After not even a month of marriage, upon the return from their honeymoon, Chiara and Enrico discovered that they were prospective parents. They received the news with joy even if they were hiding some apprehension. Chiara was still working on her degree in political science and had just enrolled in some courses. Only Enrico was working, as a physical therapist with terminally ill cancer patients. "We asked ourselves if we could succeed going forward, managing all the expenses that would be presented. However, as the Lord helped us in marriage, we were certain that He would help us also in this pregnancy."

Chiara did not have her own doctor. When it was time for her first checkup, she recalled a young couple she and Enrico had met when they were looking for a house. The wife, Daniela, was a gynecologist, and Chiara immediately found herself relating to her. "As soon as we entered their home, we felt welcome. We saw their photos of their mission in Peru, and this impressed us so much." In turn, Massimiliano, the husband, was impressed by those two young people. That evening, while taking leave of one another, he felt an impulse to give them something that might help them. Knowing that they were to be married, he gave them his wife's business card, saying, "She is a gynecologist with a specialty in obstetrics; perhaps she may be of service to you in the future." So, now pregnant, Chiara turned to Daniela.

Daniela and Massimiliano encountered Chiara and Enrico again when they came to Assisi to entrust the pregnancy into the hands of Mary in the little church of Portiuncula. They wished immediately to involve the Virgin Mary in this story. While seated in a café near the basilica that houses the little church, the couple joked that they would have waited a few months more before planning a family, just to have a little time to be newlyweds.

They were very content, but there was something in Chiara's mood that struck Daniela and worried her a little. She was expecting a baby, but she was a little grave and pensive. Daniela asked her if the pregnancy was unexpected, that perhaps it had led her to grow up in a hurry, all at once. She, however, said that with the passing of time she began to feel strange: "as if this child was not mine, as if it was not for me."

Her seriousness left us astounded, so much so that that night we could not think of anything else. In the coming days her comment kept coming back to us, like an invitation to pray for them.

The first medical appointment went well. It was the exam during the second visit, after Christmas, that Chiara's apprehension found a motive. She was in the outpatient section with her mother; Enrico, in fact, was not there. After they were married, he had begun to suffer from a toothache. An X-ray revealed a hole in his lower jaw. It was not clear if it was a tumor. Chiara was worried: that same morning they had discovered that they were expecting a baby. Knowing she was expecting and at the same time confronting the potential fear of Enrico's illness was a sudden shock for her. In reality, it was a radicular cyst, and it was removed just a few hours before Chiara's second appointment.

Initially, the exam looked good. Daniela said that she was fairly certain it was a girl and that the baby was at about fourteen weeks' gestation. While she watched the little one moving around on the screen, Daniela's expression changed suddenly. Her serene face grew very sad. Chiara was aware of it; she understood that there had to be something there, but she did not ask any questions. She asked only: "Is this the head?"—almost helping Daniela to make the diagnosis. Then, in silence, remaining calm, she waited for Daniela to say something.

With pain Daniela explained: "Look, Chiara, unfortunately there is a serious malformation that is incurable. I cannot tell you more because it is necessary to take another ultrasound at the second level in order to see the entirety of the damage and to understand if other organs are implicated."

The diagnosis was anencephaly. The baby had no skull. In this case the law permitted an abortion, defining it as therapeutic.

Pope John Paul II had written that the body "was created to transfer the hidden mystery of the eternity of God to the reality of the visible world, and thus becoming a sign of it."[5] The body says that we are made to be a gift, to give love and to receive it. In that little body that was moving in Chiara's womb was all the urgency and nobility of this mission.

Daniela asked Chiara if her husband was waiting for her outside the examining room. But she, very serene and strong,

---

[5] Semen, *La spiritualità coniugale second Giovanni Paolo II*, p. 19.

answered no. Struck by her composure, the doctor recalled that Chiara did not doubt for even a moment whether she would keep this baby.

When she left the examining room, Chiara wept in the arms of her mother, Maria Anselma, who was waiting for her in the reception area. In her head at that moment was a chorus of people all saying the same thing: *Surely you will have a healthy baby; it is expected.* But the thought that was illuminating her was quite another. "I knew that the Lord always has something different for us; not everything goes as we think. And therefore in that moment my only preoccupation was: How do I inform my husband?"

When they were engaged, they had both made the choice to live the gospel; they had received the grace to know Jesus, and they desired to encounter Him. But the concreteness of life is another matter, above all when it's necessary to say something that is terribly heartbreaking.

A few hours later, while Enrico was still in recovery, Chiara was given the more in-depth examination requested by Daniela. This time the ultrasound was three dimensional and with color. The image of Maria Grazia Letizia was crystal clear, and she could see her problem very well. The little one was lacking a skull. The doctor on duty told Chiara that if they had taken the ultrasound immediately, before all the other exams, they could have still done something.

"You mean in order to prevent the malady?" Chiara asked.

"No, in order to abort," he responded.

For Chiara, who had just seen her daughter move, it was a low blow. "It was obvious, logical, and clear that Maria would not have been able to survive after birth. However, it was also obvious that she was alive, that she was there, and that she was doing everything necessary to grow and to develop. I did not at all feel like going against her. I felt like sustaining her for as long I was able and not substituting myself for her life."

Chiara went home, alone again, because Enrico was in the hospital. He called her, but she was vague with his questions since he was still affected by the anesthesia. He wished to know if it was a boy or a girl, and for Chiara it was a relief that he did not ask anything else. She invented a story that the ultrasound machine was broken and the exam had to be postponed.

That night she could not sleep. It was a difficult moment. She asked herself why God had permitted this in her and Enrico's life. They had always sought His will. [But then] she reproached herself for having been inattentive and neglectful. She blamed herself for what had happened. She would go on with the pregnancy; about this, she had no doubt, but the doctor of the last ultrasound had looked at her as if she were mad when she told him that. The pain was great.

The next morning, she was not able to stop crying. She was aware that she could not live this suffering alone. Yet it seemed precisely what God had asked her to do. Among the questions in her head, the one that, more than all the others, threw her into desperation was precisely this: Why did God not have her discover this news together with her husband? "Why did You ask me to be the one to tell him?" she said to God. Chiara suffered for her daughter, but she had already made up her mind what to do. "Going forward with the pregnancy was clear for me; however, I did not yet have the certainty that my husband would think like this."

Finally, she cried out to God. In that difficult moment, Chiara's eyes fell on an image of the Virgin Mary, and everything changed. Peace descended on her heart. She wrote: "From being condemned to a destiny without hope, I became filled with joy in seeing how the Lord saw this suffering."

What had happened? Frightening Chiara was the fact that she and Enrico had been married for only a few months and she did not know how he would react to the news that his daughter was not well and that she would die after her birth. She feared what she would discover in Enrico's heart. Would he stop loving her? She thought: "Will my husband carry this cross, or must I carry it alone? Will he understand me?"

Looking at that image of the holy Mother of God, she remained thunderstruck. She saw herself in the Virgin Mary, in her same situation: a special pregnancy, a Son who would die before her eyes, and the weight of telling Joseph, who did not yet know anything. To both, to her and to Mary, God had asked the same thing. Little by little her horizon was transformed. "I could not ask to be able to understand everything all at once; the Lord had a plan that I could not understand."

While trying to find the words to tell Enrico about his daughter, she decided to write him a letter. She wished to tell him aloud all that was in her heart, but she knew that she could not do it; a letter would have to do it for her. In that letter to Enrico, referring to that moment of consolation, Chiara wrote: "Finally my stubborn heart has given in." That little that she had understood she gave to her husband, black on white.

She and Enrico had so wanted to be parents in a group home.[6] They had asked God to accept their desire of caring for mistreated and unloved children. "And now the Lord has responded to us," Chiara wrote. "He has given us a truly noble task; the care of a marvelous creature that many others would have hated and thrown away, left forgotten in a wastebasket in some hospital."

---

[6] A group home is a small orphanage set up for handicapped children to live in a family setting rather than in an institution.

Live and Let Yourself Be Loved

As in the episode of the cure of the official's son (see John 4:46–54), Chiara was saddened for the life of her daughter. Initially she had asked Jesus to intervene, even before knowing God's design; before knowing what He had wished to do, how He had wished to show them His love. But Jesus was teaching her how to enter into a relationship with him. Now she must simply trust in Him, allow herself to be guided, like Mary. She must learn to think of God as a person, not someone at her service. For Chiara to accept Maria Grazia Letizia was to learn true humility.

In the past, Chiara had always feared revealing herself for what she was. Before Enrico she had shown herself for the first time when, in tears, she had abandoned all hope of going forward with their love story. That choice, placed in God's hands, had led her to marriage. Now she had to go one step further. She had to go deeper. This pregnancy, which she did not for one moment consider renouncing, made her more vulnerable and exposed than ever. Exactly like her daughter, she also was a creature asking only to be loved.

Enrico's surgery concluded well. When Chiara went to pick him up at the hospital, she was tense. She wanted to cry but could not. Later in the car, her husband, unaware of everything, criticized her driving. At home she said she had to speak to him.

"Maria is not well?" he asked immediately. "Don't worry; whatever she has, we can take care of her."

"No, we cannot," Chiara responded, "because it is incompatible with life." This baby was not for them. The two embraced and cried together.

"I had never thought of this eventuality," Enrico said. "I had considered the possibility of accepting an unhealthy baby, but not that of accompanying a baby to Heaven. In that moment we discovered for the first time that we were on the same wavelength, and indeed we truly were. We knew, both of us, what to do in this situation. It was beautiful."

When Enrico spoke, Chiara heard the words that she had so desired: "Do not worry. She is our daughter. We shall accompany her as far as we can." He also did not consider refusing this gift. For Chiara it was not only the first unforgettable moment, it was the "first miracle."

Maria Grazia Letizia was an authentic gift from God, It was God who sent her in order to tell Chiara that her husband truly loved her and so that together they could say to Him: "Here I am, Lord." And He in turn, through all His infinite ways, could tell them, each day, how much He loves them.

A courtship at war led them to a marriage in peace. Once again God restored Enrico to her. And He taught them both, now more united than ever, how to accompany Maria Grazia Letizia up to the moment of letting her go.

The hope born during their engagement was not disappointed. The promise was being renewed each day, and Chiara's entrusting herself to God, in spite of her doubts, actually confronting them, bore fruit. "I thought, 'This man truly loves me ... and he loves the fruit of our love in the same way that I love her.' And from that moment grace united us all the more."

"Maria Grazia Letizia made us open our hearts," Enrico told us. "She opened the door and entered, bringing us grace and true love and teaching us the meaning of life and of eternity."

* * *

When they returned to the clinic again, this time together, they discovered the support of Daniela. She did not advise going through with the pregnancy, but as a mother, she understood their determination, and in the end she offered them her unconditional support and assistance. "She gave us so much courage," Chiara related, "because we understood that we had not only a specialist at our side, but a mother who would share with us all the challenges that we would be facing." And there were many.

For many doctors, an abortion in this case was a given. Unfortunately, it is also true for many who call themselves Catholics. There were few Christians who supported Chiara and Enrico. The fact that Maria Grazia Letizia was developing without a brain made them doubt that hers was a life in every respect. There were even those who doubted that interrupting this pregnancy could be called an abortion, as if the little one did not even exist. For Chiara and Enrico, this was their greatest pain: the harsh judgments of those around them, the advice of the persons who were close to them.

Some "Christians" were truly annoying and even mean spirited, causing them much distress. What made Chiara and Enrico suffer more was the accusation that they were not good parents. They were accused of superficiality in their judgments and in their research, including the possibility of eventual cures. Some had the nerve to tell them that the malformations in Maria Grazia Letizia were caused by some psychological block in Chiara. Others spoke of a curse and encouraged them to pray more, or at least turn to someone, a seer, with the special gifts that could liberate them.

These people caused them the greatest temptations and the most suffering. Among parishioners there were even those who accused Chiara of something that she had never said, that she herself tacitly approved of this type of abortion. It is useless to say that it was totally false. "But when the two of them turned to the Church for support," Father Vito said, "they discovered that Maria Grazia Letizia was a baby like all the others, indeed, more beautiful."

Choosing to proceed with the pregnancy, Chiara and Enrico were going forward with an idea of life that many indeed find uncomfortable. But this is precisely what the Church professes. The idea of a life that is valuable in itself proceeds from intelligence, from the capacity to reason, and from beauty. It is an idea of life that sweeps away all the world's criteria. It is an idea of life that sees that the other comes not to rob us of anything, but rather to enrich us with his presence. Father Vito had told us that the devil confuses; he places in people's heads the conviction that "children are the enemy; that a child takes life away from you, impedes you from certain existential consequences, certain career opportunities, certain emotional relationships: 'Oh God, a fourth child, how shall we manage?'" A woman who aborts is a woman who has been deceived. No child robs her of life, deprives her of a career opportunity or of self-realization. Behind the decision to abort there is a lie that is as strong and efficacious as it is hidden and unexpressed: it is the lie of the alternative.

The situation that Chiara and Enrico were living could have seemed like an option among plausible alternatives. But this story is beautiful because it immediately reveals that, in reality, there were no alternatives. Maria Grazia Letizia was not compatible with life; yes, that is true, but only with life as we understand it here.

"In the end, what could Chiara do?" Father Vito said. "She was a twenty-four-year-old who was pregnant and who let her baby develop. The baby had no brain. So what could she do? She let her grow. What is the alternative that we, instead, have put into our heads? That if you kill that baby, it no longer exists? But it is not a true alternative; it is a lie. And this is the lie: that if you kill your child, you will be happy. But it is not true; that child exists and will always exist. There is always only one thing to do, and we cause ourselves so much suffering trying to escape it. In Chiara and Enrico those truths shone in a simple way. A light shone on their faces, a light that consoled and enchanted. Exactly like the gospel, it is something that you cannot keep to yourself; you must share it and spread it.

* * *

We were at Rome when their message arrived on our cell phone. It did not exactly describe the problem, but we did not immediately call them for an explanation. We imagined that they might not have wished to speak of it on the phone, so we texted that we would arrive as soon as possible; meanwhile we would pray for them. Chiara was appreciative. She did not like to stay on the telephone, and in that moment there was an onslaught of calls that made everything more difficult.

That evening we saw each other in the little piazza of the Church of San Paolo alle Tre Fontane. Chiara was wearing a hat with a visor, and her little bump was visible by now; Enrico was still puffy from the surgery, and his eyes were glassy. We piled into the car and cried together. Chiara was very proud of Enrico for accepting his daughter and for not considering, even for a moment, refusing her.

They took advantage of the occasion to tell one another how much they loved and esteemed one another. We had the impression that Chiara's tears were not so much for Maria Grazia Letizia's situation as for the joy and happiness of having Enrico beside her.

From that moment we felt ourselves being drawn into this story and becoming an integral part of it. We told Enrico and Chiara that we would be there in prayer and in person, and we agreed with them that to love in this way was the only true possibility. We went to Mass at the Sanctuary of the Virgin of Revelation [a meeting place of the prayer group of Medjugorje] and had supper together. They told us with joy about their honeymoon and all their plans. From then on, their peace, that mysterious joy of which much would be spoken later, stunned us. While we were together, the telephone rang repeatedly. Enrico would get angry because in order to console him, people would say things that made no sense, such as: "What a misfortune. Why is this happening to you?" Chiara and Enrico felt offended because they were proud of Maria Grazia Letizia just as she was. [There was] no error in creating her. They did not think that she should be different; she was perfect for eternity.

The news began to spread that there was a special baby and two equally special parents who were accompanying her. When seeing Chiara with her pregnancy visible, people would ask if the baby was a boy or a girl, and she, without losing composure, would smile and respond, "It is a girl." Now and then someone would add that the important thing is that she is healthy. Chiara would [usually] remain calm, but sometimes she would get fed up with these ways of speaking, and they would torment her. Once she responded to a cashier: "Why? What if she is not?"—leaving the cashier speechless.

"This tells us how much we are unaccustomed to associating suffering with two happy people," Chiara explained. "We were truly happy; we were serene. No one was able to read in our faces the situation that we were confronting. The Lord was speaking through our demeanor and our faces, not so much through our words."

The special pregnancy notwithstanding, they carried on, living married life in a natural manner, like so many others. While their husbands worked, Cristiana and Chiara would keep in touch by phone, chattering in the manner of housewives. Taking on new rhythms was not easy. The days flew by without their having much success in praying; in general they seemed to accomplish little.

One day in a Catholic magazine, Cristiana found an article entitled "The Canticle of the Kitchen." There she read that marriage consecrates everything in love and that each thing done for the love of the spouse is a gift of self and more important than a thousand prayers: "I sweep the floor in gratitude for ... I make the bed as an offering for this situation," and things of this type. It immediately stirred something in Chiara that she liked very much. From that day, occupying herself with the house became a prayer. Incredibly, this type of prayer was working.

Chiara also spoke of the little controversies and affectionate squabbles with Enrico, the difficulty of keeping parents and in-laws at bay, the desire for a house of their own—in brief, the daily life of every couple.

What was extraordinary in Chiara was her docility. If you gave her advice, she would think about it, discuss it with Enrico, and try it. Leaning not on her own strengths but simply on those of the Father helped her to live what He sent her.

Chiara, who was very reserved, found herself with an enormous tummy because of the abundance of amniotic fluid, and she often felt the difficulty of having to relate the story of the baby. Sometimes she wished she could pass unnoticed, but her appearance did not make it possible. Maria Grazia Letizia wished to make herself noticed. This baby could not be hidden. "I had a belly," Chiara relates, "that forced me to witness to the greatness of the Lord."

In spite of some concerns, Chiara was doing very well. She had no difficulty sleeping during the night and scarcely noticed the weight of a task that the others struggled even to imagine.

For her it was a stupendous pregnancy every single day. She spoke to Maria Grazia Letizia with complete awareness of the situation but without the dramatic tones. Maria Grazia Letizia was very lively. "Her every little kick was a gift," Chiara liked to say. "She liked very much to be felt ... as if to remind us that she was there for us." Caressing her belly, she prayed with the baby for the various situations that became known to her and to Enrico, for persons in need. Maria's parents did everything to fuss over her and to make her feel loved.

Their serenity was like that of every other family, perhaps greater. Chiara did not envy other mothers who, unlike her, would be able to raise their children. Help, Chiara would plainly say, came from family and from friends who prayed for them. Prayer was their strength.

* * *

As the moment of birth approached, some questions emerged. There was much too much fluid: nearly six liters (in an ordinary pregnancy, there would be only one liter). If the membranes were broken abruptly, there could be hemorrhaging, a uterine atony (contraction), and another series of medical complications. Furthermore, for Chiara, the risk of dyspnea, not being able to breathe because of the pressure of the liquid, was much higher than normal.

Daniela sustained the cause of the Petrillos at Fatebenefratelli. The choice of going forward with the pregnancy required that someone among the doctors assume the responsibility for the delivery. Initially support fluctuated. Usually it was given and revoked on the basis of just one reading of the chart. But then the doctors came to know Enrico and Chiara personally and came around. The encounter was decisive.

Live and Let Yourself Be Loved

Their faces expressed a peace that left everyone disoriented, even the doctors. Looking into the eyes of one who, despite her suffering, did not detach herself from God had an effect. Knowing a couple who has Jesus as their only hope adds something to your life. Chiara and Enrico were not there to ask the doctors for an explanation of all that had happened. They were there to testify that there was no alternative to their choice, that it was not possible to make a better choice than life, that there was no other path for them. And when they smiled, everything seemed simple, logical. One of the doctors had seemed particularly motivated to deny his support. But then, finding himself in their presence, he remained silent. Having realized, among other things, that Chiara was the same age as his son, he changed his mind.

Together with the doctors, Enrico and Chiara had to choose the date of the delivery. It was not easy. "The doctors had begun to advise doing a caesarean at the thirty-fifth week," Chiara said, "because the probability that a natural birth was possible was very low."

Maria Grazia Letizia had no hypophysis, that part of the brain that could stimulate labor, and without a skull she could not make her way through the birth canal. Chiara desired so much to have a natural delivery. But Daniela made her understand that in her condition, considering also that it was her first pregnancy, the only option that she could advise was induced labor. In spite of this, Chiara continued to hope that she would at least be able to confront this travail by doing her part as a mother, up to the very end.

All mothers generate children who really do not belong to them. Being parents means precisely this. But for Chiara the awareness was even stronger. Her mission and Enrico's was immediately to accompany this baby to her encounter with God, and she wished with all her being to place herself at the best advantage to allow this to happen, so that everything could be realized according to God's plan. Thus, as she had yielded to the discovery that Maria Grazia Letizia was not healthy, and that this baby would ask only to be loved, she wished also to comply with reality and to accept the birth that the Lord would give her.

The first week of June was Chiara's last doctor appointment. Touching her belly, the gynecologist told her that she could not wait any longer; it was necessary to have Maria Grazia Letizia make her appearance. The date fixed was for June 10, Wednesday of the following week.

That day in the Morning Prayer (of the Liturgy of the Hours) there was a verse that spoke to their hearts: "Seek counsel from every wise person, and do not think lightly of any useful advice" (Tob. 4:18). They entrusted themselves to the doctor.

"That week of preparation was difficult," Chiara said, "because we knew that the moment that we were awaiting for the past eight months had arrived. We prayed together because we did not feel ready, as indeed we had not felt ready for this entire story, yet the Lord had brought us up to the eighth month of this pregnancy in serenity."

Chiara and Enrico's desire was docility to God's plan. They did not suggest to God what to do; they asked Him to prepare them. They were displeased, however, for having had to choose the day of the birth. It was a decision that created an intense interior tumult. Choosing that date coincided with the birth of Maria Grazia Letizia in Heaven. It would be the day in which they knew that they would be saying farewell to their daughter; hence, they were saddened and dejected.

A few days later, Chiara, because of her condition, was not able to attend Sunday Mass. This displeased her, and she turned to God in prayer. A little later the phone rang; it was Father Vito: "Chiara! I have just returned from New York, and I'm here at Rome. May I come and celebrate Mass at your house?"

The day before the birth, we had spoken on the phone. The next day we went to the hospital, although we were fearful of doing something inopportune. Father Vito also wished to be there and had had these same doubts. The three of us then decided to go together from Assisi to make our presence felt, even if we risked being a bother. That morning we picked up Father Vito at his residence and drove to Rome.

On June 10, the day scheduled for admission, Chiara arrived already having some contractions, to which she hadn't given much thought the previous evening. She thought perhaps that they were simply some pains, not true contractions. When the doctor examined her, he asked if she had had some pain during the week. Chiara said yes. The doctor then looked at Daniela, stunned: Chiara was already six centimeters dilated, and the birth was closer than anyone thought. Even Daniela, who was next to Enrico, understood that this was a concrete sign from God, who was present with them and doing His part.

Enrico kept us updated on the situation as we drove. He told us that Chiara was preparing to give birth alone and that the doctors now were in agreement that oxytocin, used to induce and accelerate labor, was not necessary and that they were willing to proceed with natural childbirth. It was news that gave much peace because it confirmed that the Lord Himself had chosen that day for Maria Grazia Letizia's birth. When we arrived at the hospital, the baby had not yet been born. We waited outside for her along with some relatives and friends.

With the breaking of the amniotic sac, much of the fluid emptied in a few minutes. She and Enrico told Daniela that perhaps Father Vito was already outside, ready to baptize the little one. Daniela found him in the waiting room. After quickly introducing herself, she gave him a blue smock and invited him to follow her.

Labor and birth proceeded without obstacles, leaving everyone speechless. All that was feared never occurred. Maria Grazia Letizia was born. Some of the doctors, thinking that she was already dead and not wishing to have her parents see her, immediately brought her to the neonatal island. Daniela opposed them and brought her back into the room.

When Enrico took his daughter into his arms, he felt his heart beat faster. He brought her to Chiara. They had asked the Lord for a natural birth and that Maria Grazia Letizia be born alive and thus be able to be baptized. Enrico entered and told her that it was precisely so, that Maria was still alive. And so Father Vito baptized her. For Chiara it was an unforgettable moment. "Her baptism was the greatest gift the Lord could have given us," she said. "I was looking at Enrico with our daughter in his arms: so proud of her. I was sure that she could not have had a better father."

They took photos, many photos. Enrico brought the little one outside to introduce her to her grandparents, relatives, and friends. They were deeply moved.

"Babies, at times, are entrusted to group homes for a few months or even years, but this does not impede us from loving them. Indeed we have the duty to shower them with all the love that we have, in order to 'stamp' in their memory the love that God wished to give them through our simple gestures. God will love these creatures through our deeds; therefore, we must be honored to be given so great a task." Thus, wrote Chiara in her letter to Enrico announcing the arrival of his daughter. And just forty minutes after her birth on earth, Maria Grazia Letizia was born again in Heaven.

Chiara and Enrico were truly happy. They were prepared for the worst, not for such beauty. "The moment I saw her was a moment that I shall never forget: I understood that we were linked together for life. I did not think of the fact that she would be with us so briefly. It was an unforgettable half hour.

"If I had aborted her, I do not think that I would have remembered the day of the abortion as a day of celebration, a day in which I had been liberated of something. It would have been a moment that I would have tried to forget, a moment of great suffering. But the day of Maria's birth I shall always recall as one of the most beautiful days of my life, and I shall tell all my children that the Lord wishes to send us that they have a special sister who is praying for them in Heaven.

"What I wish to say to the mothers who have lost children is this: we have been mothers; we have had this great gift. The amount of time does not matter: one month, two months, a few hours. What matters is that we have had this gift ... and it is something that can never be forgotten."

It was difficult getting a handle on the confusion of the medical personnel, each one shaken and put to the test. While some were in stunned silence over the mystery of the events, others thought that this couple was crazy, from the first of their choices to the last. But all the decisions that the others did not share, Enrico and Chiara made themselves. And this united them in a special way. For them there were no alternatives; this was the only road that God asked them to travel. They had to trust solely in Him in order to experience His grace.

"The Lord begged us not to lose faith," Enrico said. And so it was, precisely as it had happened in the time of the apostle Peter.

Later, it was Enrico who carried Maria Grazia Letizia to the mortuary.

We greeted Chiara. She was very well, as if she had not just given birth, as fresh as a rose. Some tears fell, but they were from emotion. She had an expression and a peace that was unsettling.

Chiara shared her hospital room with another mother. The woman had lost her third child in the ninth month due to a detached placenta. She was still; she would not say a word. Chiara softly informed us of her situation, asking us to pray for her. That night Chiara spoke to her. On the day that the woman was dismissed, she thanked the doctor in charge of the department, not so much for their assistance but for having put her in the same room with "that young woman who helped me to accept the death of my baby."

* * *

Two days later, June 12, there was a funeral for Maria Grazia Letizia. One would expect to see Enrico and Chiara, afflicted, sitting in one of the first pews. But one would be mistaken. They were on the same side as the chorus, playing: he on the guitar and she on the violin. And both, dressed in white (the color of the Resurrection), were singing. Seeing them like this took your breath away.

During the Prayer of the Faithful, Chiara rose and went to the pulpit. She thanked those who had accompanied them and sustained them with their prayers. She spoke of her stupor before so much love bursting from the hearts of everyone, thanks to their little daughter. She prayed for all present that the Lord would compensate them a hundredfold while they were still on this earth.

It was a very beautiful feast; the atmosphere was serene. But there were not many in the church. Most had declined to come because they did not know what to say. Thus, they lost a unique opportunity to see that Heaven can exist here on earth. Those who participated in the celebration lived a moment of eternity, a powerful experience, a proof that Paradise truly exists. Enrico and Chiara rejoiced among their tears, together with their families. Everyone was moved.

Father Vito—present once again—in his homily made referral to the burning bush [which Moses saw], a love that burns but is not consumed. Chiara and Enrico set aside their own wishes and aspirations and made space for God; "a gift from God is a gift from God, and hands off." We do not define ourselves as men or as women through our work, our house, our health, or our reputation. We define ourselves as men and women through the way we love. Maria Grazia Letizia was already ready. She already lived everything that was necessary.

At the end of the celebration, the parents approached the little white coffin at the center of the nave and accompanied it outside while everyone wept from emotion. Everything was so beautiful that we were nearly led to desire those same difficulties, in order to be able to feel the same consolation. It might be almost absurd to think that way, but that is exactly what happened. We could call it saintly envy. Enrico had prepared a prayer card with an image of the Virgin Mary holding the Infant Jesus accompanied by a message that, through their story, would become very familiar. But at that time, most of us were being introduced to it for the first time: "We are born into eternity, and we shall never die."[7]

---

[7] This statement is tied to the image of Chiara, but it was not Chiara who enunciated it. Enrico had heard the expression from a director of the religious community The Risen Jesus

Chiara Corbella Petrillo

We were content to hold you in our arms,
for even half an hour, we were fine.
We were not able to stop looking at your nose,
the same as mine,
and those little hands and those little feet.
We did not have much time to tell you too many
    things;
that we love you, we know that you know it,
but perhaps you do not know that you were born
    for eternity
and that I am not your father, nor is she your mother.
Think of it! The one who desired you is also our Father
I know it is a little complicated, but soon you will
    understand:

(Gesù Risorto), who, at the time, was terminally ill from bone
cancer. Enrico was about fifteen, and he remained impressed
by it. He repeated several times that he would like to have it
written on a T-shirt, because he felt that it was good news worth
sharing with everyone. On June 12, 2012, the day before Chiara
died, we gave Enrico, Chiara, and Francesco three T-shirts with
a blossoming sunflower and this phrase written on it.

Chiara had asked us to write a fable for Francesco that would
explain her story to him and his brothers and sisters. And the
fable was to end with the line: *We are born into eternity, and we
shall never die.*

In her last hours and immediately after, when the fable was
placed in the room where she died, next to her body and all
her photos, this saying remained engraved in the air. It was
read by everyone and rendered true by everyone — so much
so that when Enrico prepared the memorial card for Chiara's
funeral, that saying was the immediate choice. Thus, it was
truly stamped on Chiara's heart and on the hearts of the many
who had known her, either personally or because of that image.

life is marvelous;
for this also we sought you.

It does not matter how much time we spend together;
to us it matters what you shall be.
Here each thing does not matter, really;
we can make do with less of everything.
What is necessary is to know the Father;
it is to prepare ourselves for this encounter.
And you were born ready,
I do not know how to tell you how proud we are of you.
We accompanied you as far as we were able.
Now you shall know the Father,
Maria Grazia Letizia, joy of our life.

Papà Enrico and Mamma Chiara

Everything seemed incredible; in that type of situation one imagines that there is only suffering. But the young couple said no, only love counts. "With Maria Grazia Letizia," Chiara wrote, "we had the unique feeling that we had experienced eternity." With Maria Grazia Letizia, Chiara and Enrico ceased fearing death.

Chiara understood that this creature was entrusted to them by God, that the Lord placed His trust in them. From the beginning she lived her pregnancy as a privilege, a task for which she felt inadequate. When she and Enrico learned of the pathology, they also discovered that what they had seen in one another was true; it confirmed their love and united them. Living the cross together made the cross lighter, and it was beautiful.

Thanks to this daughter of silence, they learned that death was not ugly, as it had seemed to be. Grace had helped them to live this moment. Their baby had passed from their arms to those of the Father, and from this they learned how to recognize beauty. Later, when they thought back on their experience, they would continue to marvel. Here was the proof of nine, which was grace, God's strength that accompanied them during the pregnancy.

After they arrived at the cemetery of Verano, before the tomb of the little one, they sang: *When I am weak, therefore, I am strong because You are my strength* [cf. 2 Cor. 12:10]. The peace of God continued to be with them.

* * *

Just two days after the funeral, Enrico and Chiara called us, asking if they could come to our house in Assisi to rest for a few days. It had happened often, and it would continue to happen.

During that visit, we spoke much of how things had gone, of how it had been Maria Grazia Letizia and the Lord—not them and not the doctors—who had chosen the tenth of June as the date of her birth. They themselves were stunned at how happy they were.

While Cristiana washed the dishes and the husbands played and sang, Chiara rested on the divan. She had had some abdominal pains caused by the medications that she took after the delivery, but she said that she was feeling fine. Indeed, she said that she never felt better, in spite of the many around her who feared she would experience postpartum depression.

For this baby whom God had asked them to accompany as far as they could, Enrico had written a song. He wrote it in one hour, when they did not yet know of the malformation. When he reread it, a feeling of melancholy came over him: "It is beautiful," he said, "but it seems to contain something else." Time would confirm it. For them that song was prophetic. It is entitled "So Much Love":

> You are the only one for me.
> You take me by the hand and bring me far away,
> Sadness leaves me.
> You love me.
>
> I would like to be reborn from the height of your
> spirit.
> How it can be I do not know.
> But to live together in every instant that remains
> to me
> Would be like not dying anymore.
>
> This flower that is born speaks to me of you.
> You are the only love for me.
> You will love me always with a love greater
> Than me. I have been created by you. So much love
> So much love, so much love,
> So much love is there for you.

Is it possible to walk the same path as Enrico and Chiara? Yes, if one knows the secret: to say yes each day to your story; to trust in Jesus, who tells you: "Do not fear."

Become children of God. In reality we already are. The problem is that we do not know it.

What Chiara and Enrico discovered is that God never disappoints. In recalling the teaching of St. Francis (of Assisi) according to whom, the contrary of love is not hate but possession, Enrico said: "Our prayer was that we would not possess the life of Maria, that we would instead accompany her as far as we were able. I am truly proud of my daughter because she was born ready. Is not the objective of our life, sooner or later, the encounter with Jesus Christ? I ask myself: can it be a misfortune that she is already there?"

3

No Imperfection

Before I formed you in the womb I knew you,
and before you were born I consecrated you;
I appointed you a prophet to the nations.

—Jeremiah 1:5

November 19, 2009, just five months after Maria's birth, Enrico and Chiara presented their testimony at one of the encounters—part of the series *In the World but Not of the World*—sponsored by the Science and Life Association of Rome. The title was truly perfect, because Enrico and Chiara did not share with the world of their friends and relatives the need to know, at all costs, what was behind Maria Grazia Letizia's situation: what her birth signified and what God's motive was in permitting her underdevelopment. They had simply accepted her without questions or analyses, only gratitude. But the battle continued to unfold all around them, so [in the end], they accepted the invitation to present their story publically in order to verify it.

Together with the Science and Life Association, the event was organized by the Christian Association of Italian Workers (Acli) and the parish of St. Frances of Rome at Ardeatino (Santa Francesca Romana all'Ardeatino). On the dais with [Chiara and Enrico] were Daniela, Dr. Noia of the Quercia Millenaria Association,[8] and Gianluigi DePalo. It was DePalo who thought up the idea of the encounter, thinking that they had a miracle to share. He considered them perfect witnesses of that prophetic thinking that brings Heaven down to the earth. Between the DePalo Family and the Petrillos a great friendship had developed during Chiara's pregnancy with Maria Grazia Letizia.

It was the first time that husband and wife gave a public testimony, and there was surprise. Chiara demonstrated an ability to speak before the little crowd that gathered to listen to them as if it were a common occurrence. She narrated the story of Maria Grazia Letizia from the first medical appointment to the birth with consistency and spontaneity and without one word too many.

At the end, her husband furnished the letter: "Without God, everything becomes a mishap," but with God you can see the suffering as an invitation to dance, and if "you begin to dance, you become aware that yes, suffering is there, but there is also much joy and much peace." What was supposed to be a simple speech was transformed into an act of faith in God, who does not abandon and who fulfills His promises.

Those present remained completely amazed. Some of the statements that Chiara made that evening were received as if they were sculpted in stone. One among many: "The Lord puts the truth inside each one of us, and there is no possibility of misunderstanding it."

In his Gospel, Mark tells how Jesus reproached the disciples when He saw them chase away some children who were

---

[8] Quercia Millenaria Association was founded in 2005 as a center of assistance to sustain families living through pathological pregnancies and terminal fetuses.

gathering around Him. Two thousand years ago, from a social point of view, babies did not count for anything. But if we think seriously about it, our time is not so different from the time of Jesus. And with the arrival of a new life, many act like the disciples: they are alarmed by the agitation it causes and think that it would be better to reject it.

To abort is to give back a gift. The eternity of God wishes to burst in upon the daily reality of time precisely through that child, who is one of God's words, written in his own hand [in the book of life]. The parents who accept a baby accept God. In accepting Maria Grazia Letizia, Chiara and Enrico did more. Like the Virgin, who, in the words of Chiara, accepted like a gift "a Son who was not for her, a Son who would die, a Son who would die in her presence [as she stood] under the Cross," Chiara and Enrico were saying yes to a mission that would go well beyond themselves.

The words of that testimony, pronounced with a gentle but decisive voice, were so powerful that they stirred up a conversion in many of those present, going so far as to convince other parents in the same situation to do the same. It was not possible to pretend that you had never before heard what they were saying: they were confirming what Jesus said in the Gospels.

Enrico concluded his talk by recalling that Chiara, upon returning home after the birth of Maria Grazia Letizia, had said, "You know, I would do it again."

On the evening of that encounter, Chiara was already pregnant with Davide Giovanni.

* * *

After a first case of anencephaly, the recurrence of the pathology is more probable. During the summer, Chiara underwent the normal examinations, where attention was also paid to the factors that could have caused the malformation. In view of a second pregnancy, the doctors told her that a major dose of folic acid would help reduce the risks.

Just enough time had elapsed to allow Chiara's body to recuperate from the pregnancy. She and Enrico felt that waiting to have another child would be ceding to the lie or refusing a grace. They asked themselves: "But why is it necessary to wait? Must we cry and mourn?"

They then experienced a great joy, a consolation that overwhelmed the sadness. They did not wish to deny themselves a grace that God wished to give them; they desired a new pregnancy. Already at Medjugorje, where they went during the summer with Father Vito, to give thanks for the birth of Maria, they asked God for another child.

After they returned from that trip, they were even happier. They told us of the testimony they heard from Mirjana, one of the seers of Medjugorje. Chiara was particularly struck when she told her how even though she loves her husband and her children very much, she always struggles to "remain" on earth and not go immediately to Gospa (the Virgin).[9] This gave Chiara enormous peace and even more, the certainty that for her daughter, she could not have asked better.

Love could not wait. Davide Giovanni arrived immediately. When she discovered that she was expecting again, Chiara already knew what to do. The first ultrasound scan went well. The Petrillos awaited each appointment with a little bit of fear, but also with incredible trust.

---

[9] *Gospa* is the term the seers of Medjugorje used to refer to the Virgin Mary.

No Imperfection

And then with the second ultrasound, at the end of December, an agitated Daniela was able to see the entire head of the little one. It seemed that everything was okay; the anencephaly was not represented. Everyone was happy and relieved—so much so that many began to speak of Davide as the child of consolation. Enrico and Chiara often heard people say: "You shall see that this child will be a great joy." It was a comment that caused them acute suffering, especially when related by people close to them. "It was as if Maria was a child we must forget," Enrico explained.

Daniela scheduled the third ultrasound at Fatebenefratelli with another colleague. Chiara was entering more deeply into her life, and she feared that she was too involved; for a doctor this is a risk.

On January 19, 2010, the day of the examination, Daniela was forced to remain at home, but in trepidation. She waited for a telephone call that never seemed to come. She kept asking herself how the exam would go. Agitated, she decided to call, but no one in the clinic responded. A few hours later, one of her colleagues finally called her, the one who did the ultrasound. "Davide was missing one leg and the other had only a stump." Those words froze time.

From the Church of St. Frances of Rome, the one Enrico and Chiara had chosen as their parish, the news spread quickly. Father Fabio Rosini, the pastor, asked for prayers for a young couple called upon to confront a difficult trial for the second time in the course of just a few months. He added that something of greatness was occurring, that through the lives of these two young people and their children, God was speaking. Many of those who knew them, and were profoundly saddened, would be called upon to open themselves up to grace.

This time the diagnosis was a disability. "Where are you taking us?" Chiara and Enrico asked God when they discovered that Davide was ill, that he had a malformation of the legs. "The first time, with Maria," Chiara said, "the Lord asked us: 'Are you willing to accompany a child even to where I ask you and no further?' We did, and it was beautiful. The second time with Davide, He asked: 'Are you prepared to accept a disabled child into your family, even one with serious problems?' Also in that case we said yes, as in response to a gift of grace that had preceded us."

[In order] to understand if there was an underlying problem, some type of genetic defect at the source that could explain the development of the pathologies in Chiara's womb, she and Enrico agreed to undergo specific examinations. They did not wish these examinations to be the excuse for telling them what to do, but they gave in to the pressure of those around them who desired more knowledge. "So that you may be more tranquil," the others told them. "To make us cease choosing life," they responded. But if they were to discover genetic problems, Chiara and Enrico would simply be more aware of the risk, not disposed to choose differently.

The response was clear. There was nothing that could explain the pathology; the malformation was completely accidental. There was no link between the two pregnancies. "It never rains; it pours" was among the comments of the geneticist. They were the results that definitively released Chiara and Enrico from the grip of those who, in a veiled manner, were advising them to turn away from choosing life. "What kind of a solution would it be?" Enrico asked himself. "God created life for eternity, and I should tell Him no?"

Chiara and Enrico were preparing themselves to accept Davide Giovanni. Enrico immersed himself in the world of the disabled and became an expert on prostheses for the legs. Helping him out a great deal was Nick Vujicic, an extraordinary young man born without arms or legs. The film *The Butterfly Circus*, in which he starred, moved them and all their friends.

In February Chiara had her fourth ultrasound. Next to her was Enrico. He and Daniela had their eyes fixed on the monitor. There was another doctor involved in the exam, but Daniela was there with them as a friend. The ultrasound immediately revealed the problem: there was no fluid.

This changed everything once again. Besides legs, Davide Giovanni was also missing kidneys, and as a consequence his lungs could not develop enough to allow him to breath. Thus, the diagnosis included multiple visceral malformations to the pelvis (bladder and kidneys) together with the absence of the lower limbs. He, like his sister, would not survive.

Chiara was on the examining table with her belly uncovered. She received the news remaining calm in her faith and keeping her composure, and then two tears gave truer evidence of her feelings.

After the exam, Chiara and Enrico left, stopping on their way to pray in the nearby Church of Sant'Anastasia (next to the Circus Maximus) that hosted the perpetual Eucharistic adoration and where they once again handed over their child to the Most Holy One.

Chiara loved to repeat that where all the others saw something extraordinary, she had not done anything special there. Her smile said, "I don't understand, but I accept." Both she and Enrico would say that it cost them much to give back Davide Giovanni. Again she found herself before something much greater and different from what she had desired. For her it was a hard blow.

Chiara Corbella Petrillo

Chiara had always had a frank relationship with the Lord. Whatever she was living she placed before the Father without too many problems. But the incredible thing was her capacity to make space. During those years, she made her way through the same questions, the struggles and the hopes of every other woman. The difference was that she allowed herself to change plans radically and to accept the new occurrences, always certain that the Father gives only good things to His children.

Chiara's smiles were always followed by authentic confrontations and battles between her desire for a normal life and the will of the Father, in whom she found her joy. And if those disputes with her Lord, which were so direct and so intense, had involved any of us, they would have lasted much longer. For her, they usually lasted only one night.

The malformation of Davide Giovanni was very disabling. And although after Maria Grazia Letizia, both Enrico and Chiara felt ready to accept a child with his problems, precisely out of love for him, they also asked God to make him capable of carrying his cross — or to take it away from him.

"We must not be possessive," Enrico said. "We do not have the right of life over others, period. The Lord is giving me a cross; I must take it up, because in that cross I will discover something that the Lord wishes to say to me."

As soon as they had received the news, together with Daniela, they went to Gubbio to meet with Sister Chiara — of the nuns of Bethlehem — who had prayed for them. When they returned to Rome, we met them at a restaurant and had a long talk.

From their words we understood that they were wondering what the Lord had in mind for them. They were disappointed obviously, but they never posed the idea of refusing the baby. They were resolved to prepare themselves to accept him.

No Imperfection

Simone then said that evidently Maria Grazia Letizia had gone to Jesus recommending the Petrillos as parents for little Davide, saying that they would certainly accept him and give him all that was necessary on earth and for Heaven. The Petrillos looked at each other as if they had received good news. Chiara smiled and brightened.

Guiding Chiara's journey the entire distance, especially what seemed the most absurd part, was the hand of God. As a result, Enrico and Chiara were able to carry this cross in peace. Davide Giovanni's complex pathology, which did not even have a name, was much rarer than that of Maria Grazia. But this pregnancy was received with the same gratitude and serenity as the first. To anyone who asked news of her pregnant abdomen and her plans for the summer, Chiara was once again able to respond with a smile that, after the birth, Davide Giovanni had an appointment in Paradise.

In order to speak of the serenity that surrounded their presence, it was enough to recall that they did not wish to spend their time alone feeling sorry for themselves. Rather, they continued to demonstrate openness and a baffling hospitality, always offering themselves to others. And the others could only profit from it. Already in the days immediately following the diagnosis, whoever called on them at home experienced a peace that allowed God to enter their hearts. The smile, the sweetness, and the beauty of Chiara were as far as could be from the desperation of a person who thinks only of her own pain. Truly the hand of God was in all this.

Not long after their situation was known, Father Vito visited them from Assisi. Chiara greeted him with joy. She was always happy to see him. To her he was a man of God, who knew how to simplify things and to offer the right guidance. Father Vito spent the entire day with them. Once again they found themselves having to decide how to confront this new birth from Heaven. They were hours of profound sharing.

In contradiction to the celebration of life was the recurring accusation put forth precisely after the discovery that Davide Giovanni would not survive. It was the ancient and diabolical charge that the sin of the parents is visited upon the children, or that if God does not heal, it is because the one who asks does not truly have faith. Davide Giovanni's malady was, therefore, the fault or sin of Enrico and Chiara.

"Those accusing us did not do it in bad faith; unfortunately, many people truly believed it," Enrico recalled. "A magical faith is difficult to put up with. It is one in which you manage the faith; you use God to make Him do whatever you wish; you believe that God can truly be used this way."

For Enrico and Chiara, the reason for this attitude was simple: "In effect, it is the refusal of the cross. You wish to find a solution for the cross." And this solution is always the same: the healing of the body. But God cannot allow us to forget that we are created for eternity.

"One may ask for a cure for his illnesses, but the one who demands a cure has lost his way," Enrico continued. "Here, it is Satan who is speaking to you of God. But truly he cannot speak of God; he can only try to hide from you that you are a child of God. The fact that Jesus Christ is in Heaven tells you that you are a child of God. What Satan does not let you see is eternity, which comes after. He obscures your view, so that you see solely this world; he does not speak to you of God but of a half god. He has deceived you."

The cross cannot be avoided; because of this, Jesus made it his. "Standing before the cross is truly difficult." But you make it

No Imperfection

much more difficult by refusing it, [because] then He will compel
you to take it up.

* * *

It has been beautiful accompanying you even if at times
it seemed to us that you were leading us along your path;
You spoke to us of Him
and of His motherly love, of the wheat grain,
and of the love you cherish.
You taught us that love does not create
anything imperfect; you are a wonder,
unique, unrepeatable, and marvelous.
How much love you have given us!
I am happy to be your brother,
although, I have discovered that I am also
for a bit your father, and you are also
my son, but it is a mystery too great
to follow fully.
Of one thing I am certain: you are destined
for a glory greater than ours.
Who knows what you will do,
who knows what you will do,
little Davide?
I do not know why Jesus wished to remain
yet a little with us.
You were great; you told us
only toward the end that in you was He.
But now that we know it
we no longer fear letting you go;
you go: we shall accompany you
with a glance, my love, go. . . .

Go to see what is beyond the mountains,
there is a beautiful surprise awaiting you.

They are the words that Enrico wrote for Davide Giovanni's memorial card. They testify to the times in which, initially, he and Chiara were thinking of accepting a disabled child into their family after the discovery that Davide Giovanni would not survive.

But above all they gave witness to the awareness that God is alive and powerful. Enrico and Chiara knew it. The Lord was present in their life; they felt Him close. "It is something that increased within us; the Lord planted the seed, then He watered it well," Enrico said. "You have the experience of Maria Grazia Letizia, this daughter who went away to Heaven after half an hour, and even before that, the pregnancy itself, those nine marvelous months.... During those years everything defied human logic. And it was precisely this, in a manner, that helped us to increase our communion with Jesus. While everything burned, inside you felt refreshed. While you danced this dance with Jesus, which is suffering, you asked yourself: 'But I am at peace. How is it possible?'"

When God revealed to them that Davide Giovanni would not live and that he was also ready for Heaven, Enrico and Chiara had already had this experience. They trusted in God; they were not downcast. "It will not discourage us." And thus it happened again.

That spring there was an exposition of the Holy Shroud in Turin, where it is kept. We did not have to think twice; the four of us (five with Davide Giovanni) planned our visit. The trip began with that prayer that had been written by Sister Chiara for the ordination of Father Vito. We did not know the prayer;

we learned it while on our way, by listening to it pronounced, phrase by phrase, and then repeating it. But, phrase by phrase, we had the impression that we needed a lot of courage to pray it. It was an act of consecration to Mary. Chiara was very serene and secure while speaking: *Totus tuus* (all yours). This is how the Petrillos began their days, giving themselves completely to God through the hands of Mary.

On that same occasion, we spoke of widowhood. Chiara asked Cristiana if she thought a young spouse should remain alone until the very end. It seemed to her to be asking too much.

We spoke of many other things, we sang, and we planned trips together and concerts to attend. After we arrived at Turin, all our dear friends, whom Chiara and Enrico were meeting for the first time, gave us a great welcome. All, indeed, knew of the Petrillos. Chiara and Enrico were tenderly moved by all the affection and kindness shown to them.

The day of the visit to the Shroud was extremely important. There was a long line, and Chiara, with her pregnant belly, had some pain. Because of her, although she objected, we asked to go ahead of the others in line.

As a prompt for our prayer before the Shroud, Father Vito gave us some input by phone: "More than the Passion, it is an occasion for meditation on the Resurrection. Those wounds of love brought Him to life."

When we reached the Shroud we were speechless. That mad love shocked us. We stood before it in prayer.

After we left the church, we spoke of what we had just experienced and seen. The Petrillos told us that they asked for the healing of their little one but especially for the grace to have a heart ready to accept him and to receive, this time also, a great gift. "The Acts of the Apostles tells us that just the shadow of

Peter was enough to cure someone; here we had the shadow of Jesus!" To see those wounds transformed into an embrace gave them courage in their difficulties, reminding them of what they had already lived and preparing them for the next step.

* * *

This time Chiara's abdomen was very small. In the ultrasounds the baby was always less visible because of the small amount of amniotic fluid. This time, also, it was necessary to schedule the delivery. It was necessary to "bring" Davide Giovanni into the world, and it was not possible to wait too long. The doctors feared complications. For Chiara there was the risk of infections and for Davide Giovanni death in the uterus or a breech birth, a more difficult birth. Daniela wished to be there at all costs. Once again she felt that it would concern something great and beautiful.

Chiara, on her part, felt that in the last year and a half God had accompanied her and her husband in an extraordinary way. She could not have been more grateful for all this.

The doctors, Daniela included, wished to bring forward the baby's birth. They spoke of it to Chiara and Enrico. On June 23 Daniela took them aside. She wished to convince them that it was better this way; she looked for rational and convincing reasons that they could accept. But the look on Chiara's face was eloquent and persuasive. She wished to wait; she did not want to decide the day. If she did so, it would deprive her son of a part of his journey—the journey on which the Lord had asked her and her husband to accompany him.

When they left each other, nothing had been decided. They said that they must meet again. Daniela went home agitated. Only that evening did she find a little peace toward midnight, when she sent a message to Chiara, telling her that she was now persuaded and that they would do as Chiara wished. Together they would wait for a sign indicating the completion of time for Davide, just as it had happened with Maria Grazia Letizia. In that case God had not disappointed. Why should He do so now?

Chiara responded to her with another message: "Thank you, Dani. We are sure that also this time He will make us understand what we must do. If it is to be Wednesday, He will not make us wait. We are serene. Before being our son he belongs to Him. Good night and thank you truly." A few hours later, her contractions began.

It was five o'clock in the morning when Daniela's phone rang. It was Enrico, to say that the moment for the appointment at Fatebenefratelli was here. When Chiara arrived, she was at four centimeters and the contractions were still irregular. There was enough time for her and Enrico to go the hospital chapel to pray. Meanwhile Daniela alerted the entire team. Incredibly, it was the same that exactly a year ago assisted at the birth of Maria Grazia Letizia.

When they were going up to the delivery room, Chiara was having stronger contractions. This time Daniela convinced her to take oxytocin and to have an epidural anesthesia. She wanted to employ everything that would be helpful in managing the delivery.

At six in the morning Cristiana and I also received a call from Enrico. Incredibly, Chiara was in the delivery room. We rushed to pick up Father Vito, and we made it to Rome in a flash. Enrico kept us informed step by step of each change. These early-morning races in the car with Vito would become a ritual.

A few hundred meters from the hospital, along the Lungotevere Boulevard, traffic was paralyzed. Enrico had just called to say that Davide was being born. There was a moment of panic [in the car]: Father Vito had to be there for the baptism.

Simone, with his usual calm, said to him: "Stop a motor scooter and make him give you a lift."

And immediately Cristiana said: "What are you saying ..."

Father Vito, however, had already opened the door to stop the first passing motor scooter. What an absurd scenario. The fellow on the scooter looked at him suspiciously.

"Ciao. There's a woman in the hospital giving birth. The baby will not live long, and I must baptize him. Will you give me a ride to the Isola Tiberina?"

The fellow murmured yes, slightly convinced.

"What is your name?"

"Francesco."

"Perfect!" Padre Vito said to him, smiling. And so we watched him distancing himself from us with his habit flying about in the faces of the other drivers.

This time the pediatrician was already informed of the situation. He knew that the parents wished the baby to be baptized. Davide Giovanni was also ready. Only Chiara did not feel ready, but Father Vito spoke to her and blessed her. From that moment a new peace came over her.

When Davide was born, he was received in silence. Daniela said to give him, with the umbilical cord still attached, to the mother, and she received him, embracing him tenderly. "My son, my love," she whispered to him.

He was a baby who was dying. Everything happened in silence in a stirring sweetness.

Between Chiara and her children there was a special rapport. They were opening the path to Heaven for her. What secrets they must have exchanged.

No Imperfection

The family remained alone together: Chiara, Enrico, and Davide Giovanni. His heart contracted and expanded in breaths ever more copious, slowly chasing away the fear of death and the suffering of life.

It was time for Father Vito to enter and baptize him. The grandparents, some relatives, we (Simone and Cristiana), and other friends came to meet him. Davide Giovanni, like his sister a year before, was born again in Heaven: his life on this earth lasted thirty-eight minutes. Also on this occasion, the time was not brief; it was full.

Davide was one of the most beautiful babies we had ever seen; with his delicate features, little curls, and chubby hands. His serene little face infused a great peace in you. As we spoke of all this to Enrico, who was happy that we noticed, he responded: "Have you seen how beautiful he is? He is perfect!"

Enrico and Chiara, although with eyes a bit shiny, were well —happy and transformed by that love.

The little one was cleaned and dressed. Enrico placed a tau (T-shaped cross) at his neck—like the one he had given his sister—then once again he went downstairs and brought his baby in his arms to the mortuary.

This time, since there were no complications, Chiara was able to go home immediately. Two hours after giving birth, she was already outside with a bottle of Gatorade in hand, serene and smiling, full of joy for having known her son.

Before this birth Chiara and Enrico were asked how it would be this time, so similar to what they had already experienced. They discovered that it was different, just as the love for each child is different: "Outside the hospital we were walking and saying to each other, 'Have we truly just greeted our son?' " Each moment spent with them filled us with their love.

"Our faces were filled with joy," Chiara related. When speaking of the pregnancies and births of Maria Grazia Letizia and Davide Giovanni, she did so as if both she and her husband had physically accomplished them together.

Those who were either with them or heard from them that day, June 24 (which was among others also the birthday of Father Vito), were able to witness how content and grateful to God they were for the beauty that they had again savored.

Then on June 26, the same month and in the same church where the funeral of Maria was offered, that of Sant'Angelo in Pescheria, a service was held. However, at Davide Giovanni's funeral there were even fewer people. Along the way, old friends and acquaintances had dispersed and were replaced by all those present; nearly all were new "traveling companions." After the testimony at the Church of Santa Francesca Romana, God had given them many new friends. Chiara and Enrico felt as if some of them had been with them for a lifetime. All gave them their strongest support and loyal companionship. Through them, they received not only affection but that grace from God with which Chiara and Enrico were so in love.

It was the most beautiful experience, another funeral demonstrating eternal life. Although the road up to this moment was a path full of uncertainties, it was precisely through this that God was able to reveal a surprising and unexpected grace: "We were able to think of the births of Davide and Maria as great miracles," Chiara said, "one more beautiful than the other."

Chiara and Enrico, once again in the chorus, played and sang. In his homily Father Vito seized upon the paradox of [Chiara and Enrico] finding themselves in the same situation exactly one year later: an absurdity through which God speaks and in which those present are fortunate to be involved. He said that Chiara

No Imperfection

and Enrico were like the Shroud in which one can choose to see only the signs of the Passion or those also of the Resurrection.

The God of Christians is a God who surprises and at times frightens. They see Him walk like a ghost on the sea, even inviting them to enter into the storm. They see Him humiliate the wise with two pregnancies that, as has been certified, were independent of each other. They see Him teach the great in the figure of a baby who weighs only one kilogram and seven hundred grams (slightly over three pounds). They see Him lay bare the hearts of adults with a life that lasts just half an hour.

This, continued Father Vito, is a baby come to redeem everything that has been scorned and accused of being useless. That is our life when we consider it with the eyes of the world. To Davide, as to us, there was nothing lacking; there was no oversight on the part of God.

During the Prayer of the Faithful, Chiara got up and went to the pulpit. She prayed for all the mammas present there and those who would be [mammas]. She prayed that the Lord would illuminate their mission. Gratitude, tears, joy, and consolation: once again a funeral became proof that Paradise exists.

At the end of the Mass, Chiara approached Cristiana with a great smile and whispered to her, "Are you happy?" Cristiana said yes. And she responded: "So am I, nearly more so than on our wedding day!" It stunned her at first.

This time also, at the end of the liturgy, Enrico and Chiara walked the central nave, carrying the little coffin of their son, accompanying him outside the church, passing before a poster that was next to the photo of Davide Giovanni, declaring what God had stirred up in the hearts of his young parents: which is, Enrico related, that "the most important goal of life is to be loved. The important thing is not to do something but to be born, to let ourselves be loved." The goal of life is to discover that we are children who are loved. It is this that gives peace.

"*Peace be with you,*" Pope Francis said. "This is not a greeting nor even a simple good wish: it is a gift, indeed, *the* precious gift that Christ offered his disciples after he had passed through death and hell." (Regina Caeli, April 7, 2013). Peace is experienced by the one who allows himself to be loved.

* * *

On March 12, 2010, Chiara wrote:

Who is Davide?

A little one who received as a gift from God a very important role: that of knocking down the great Goliaths that are inside each one of us—knocking down our power as parents as we make decisions about him and for him. He showed us that he would grow and that he was like this because God had need of him like this.

He knocked down our "right" to desire a child that was for us, because he was only for God.

He knocked down the desire of those who called him a child of consolation, the one who would make us forget the sorrow of Maria Grazia Letizia.

He knocked down the trust in the statistic that claimed we had the same probability of having a healthy child as anyone else.

He unmasked the magical faith of the one who thinks he knows God and then asks Him to be the candy vending machine.

He demonstrated that God performs miracles, but not with our logical limitations, because God is something greater than our desires (he knocked down the idea of those who seek not salvation of the soul in God but only that of the body; of all those who ask God for a happy and simple life that does not at all resemble the life of the cross that Jesus left us).

Davide, so little, hurled himself with strength against our idols and cried out with strength in the face of those who did not wish to see; he forced so many to run for shelter in order not to recognize their defeat.

And I thank God for my having been defeated by little Davide; I thank God that the Goliath that was inside me is now finally dead, thanks to Davide. No one has succeeded in convincing me that what was happening was a misfortune, that it derived from the fact that we were distancing ourselves from God, even if only unconsciously. I thank God that my Goliath is finally dead and that my eyes are free to look beyond and to follow God without having fear of being what I am.

Chiara, like the paralytic at the pool of Bethsaida, was living the cure of the will (cf. John 5:1–18). Little Davide brought her to a maturation of faith. God was always in control; there was no error. The body of Davide was a form of His love, an indication of the particular way in which only He can love.

> You have spoken to us of Him
> and of His motherly love,
> of the wheat grain
> and of the love you cherish.
> You taught us that love does not create
> anything imperfect.

Davide Giovanni incarnated the parable of the wheat grain that must die in order to bear fruit. He had in a way preannounced what would happen to Chiara: Davide Giovanni was truly a prophet. Not by chance was he born on June 24, the feast day of St. John the Baptist.

Chiara also wrote: "If Davide could have spoken, he would have said, 'I am splendid.'"

4

Francesco and the Dragon

Truly, truly, I say to you, unless a grain of wheat
falls into the earth and dies, it remains alone;
but if it dies, it bears much fruit.

—John 12:24

When listening to God, it is necessary:
to accept not understanding,
to be disposed to suffer, to renounce
evil, that is, to choose [the good].

—From Chiara's notes

There is one fact more than any other that demonstrates the disconnection between the pathologies of the two babies, Maria Grazia Letizia and Davide Giovanni. More than their rarity—for the first, one can speak of one case in two thousand; for the second, there is not even a name—is the fact that Chiara became pregnant again, and this time the baby was healthy. This did not, however, satisfy the so-called disinterested parties, not even with verification from geneticists.

A few months after the birth and demise of Davide Giovanni, Chiara and Enrico's desire for a new pregnancy was great, but there were many external pressures. "So many told us to abandon the idea of having our own children," Chiara said. "Others told us that it was better to allow at least a year to pass before trying again. But each time we thought of having to wait in order to content those around us, we felt empty and sad." Chiara and Enrico looked at each other and asked each other: "But why should we wait?" They decided to entrust their dream to the one who knew how to guard it and to defend it better than any other: to the Virgin Mary. If this desire came from God, they thought, no one would be able to take it away from them or prevent it from being accomplished.

The citation that Chiara would use as a lamp guiding her steps, shining more brightly than ever, was that if God opens, no one can close. "Thus," Chiara explained, "while making a tour of the Seven Churches we decided to entrust this desire to God, so that it was He who would guide us with His wisdom and His response did not allow us to wait. It seemed that we were literally a threesome again!"

The pilgrim tour of the Seven Churches is one of the most beautiful pilgrimages one can possibly make at Rome. The participants walk the nearly twenty kilometers (12.5 miles) at night, visiting the seven jubilee basilicas of the city (among them, St. Peter, St. Paul outside the walls, and St. Mary Major). This special devotion takes place twice a year, in May and in September. It is associated with the name of St. Philip Neri, but it was not he who invented it. In reality the saint took up this ancient tradition and gave it a vigor it had never known before. Chiara and Enrico chose September in which to make their presentation.

At Santa Maria Maggiore (St. Mary Major), which contains the relics of a portion of Jesus' manger, Enrico asked for the gift of another child. A few days later, Chiara was newly pregnant.

Francesco and the Dragon

Chiara, who, when she had important things to say, took pen to paper, wrote to her doctor, who had always supported her and who, she was sure, would support her this time. Daniela was, by now, a friend. She had accompanied the births of Maria Grazia Letizia and of Davide Giovanni. She had gone beyond the role of responsible medical doctor (Chiara had already said publically that for them she was the most important doctor in the world). To Daniela she confided her shock of such an "immediate response" on the part of God.

"Before knowing whether it was male or female," Chiara noted, "Enrico said: 'We shall call this one Francesco.'"

The Petrillos did not hide their preoccupations; they knew too well that they could be facing new malformations. But they were serene and in peace as always. Enrico would even let loose with a comment or a joke, making light of the suffering they had experienced so many times. Once, at the house of friends, he said: "Maria was missing a head; David, legs.... Let's see ... what's with the third one?" For those around him, liberating laughs were hands off, but for him, who had always been capable of calling things by their name, it was completely natural.

A little before discovering she was expecting again, Chiara was aware of an aphtha (a small white ulcer) on her tongue. Initially she did not give it much thought, but with the passing weeks the aphtha did not go away; indeed, it worsened. So she began to make the rounds trying to understand its cause: first, it was the dentist, then the dermatologist, and finally the otolaryngologist (ear and throat specialist), who advised her to have a biopsy of the lesion.

Meanwhile Francesco was growing in her belly, and he was well. Daniela said that she had never seen ultrasounds so clear and so beautiful as those of the little Petrillo at eight weeks.

Chiara was happy. Enrico joked: "If it was enough to call him Francesco, the Lord should have told us with the first one!"

Rarely are the results of biopsies imprecise. But this was the case with Chiara. Hers were not diagnosable. Chiara would have to be examined periodically. During the successive visits with the otolaryngologist, the doctor saw that the lesion was enlarging and that it had all the characteristics of requiring immediate removal. They decided not to wait.

Chiara called Daniela and told her that she would have to be operated on in just two days, March 16, 2011, and with little Francesco still in her belly. It was the first of two phases of the surgery. For the second phase, it was necessary to wait until after Francesco's birth. Stunned by the news, Daniela gathered her courage and, although not acquainted with him, telephoned the surgeon engaged for the operation.

Looking back to those moments, it is evident that Chiara was being prepared for more than what she would live through in just a little while. Everything was needed to prepare her for her encounter with God.

"You believe it is a carcinoma, right?" she asked Daniela as a doctor.

"It is a carcinoma," she heard her respond.

In the days preceding the operation, Chiara did everything to avoid worrying those around her. She never complained, and she faced each difficulty with a smile. Her simplicity was disarming. No one around her understood exactly what it concerned. Whoever met her and Enrico during that period continued to experience the good that came with their company. Chiara could have poured out her troubles on everyone; instead, anyone who called on her was able to lean on her fragility and receive words of comfort. She turned no one away and considered each one's needs. Like St. Francis, she also was endowed with exquisite and rare discernment (insight), "taking into consideration each one's situation."[10] Whoever visited the Petrillos always returned home consoled and grateful.

Roberto, Chiara's father, remembers how his daughter had always made atypical and uncommon situations normal for him and his wife. Even as a child she had the capacity to enter into the heart of others, to draw out the best in them, constantly placing herself at the service of others. And her cheerfulness remained intact even up to this latest challenge. Indeed, she showed more strength than ever.

On March 16, Daniela was with Chiara. She had succeeded in finding a substitute for her shift at the hospital. Although Chiara and Enrico told her not to worry, that she had already done so much for them, she was not able to remain serene staying away. She understood that she would be able to be a little company for Enrico, who was waiting and praying outside the operating room.

When she arrived at the hospital, she found Chiara and Enrico already in the room alone. They greeted each other, and then they all began to pray together. Given the hour, they prayed the Morning Prayer, following the Liturgy of the Hours that they had learned to recite at Assisi; after this, they chatted and waited for Chiara to be called to the operating room for the surgery. Like the friends they were, they continued talking and even joking, as if it were an ordinary situation and everything was normal. Daniela told Chiara not to worry, that she would keep Enrico company. Then the doctors called her. The moment had arrived.

[10] *Fonti Francescane*, 288, n. 421.

Outside the operating room, the surgeon asked the gynecologist if she also wished to be with Chiara. Daniela did not expect it, but with a swift, almost reflexive response, she said yes.

"I had not even minimally considered it," she related. "Usually when they see me, young and female, they do not even take me for a medical doctor; so the offer took me by surprise."

The surgeon considered her presence beneficial to Francesco. She would be able to stand next to Chiara to monitor the baby's heartbeat.

Daniela found a smock and entered the room. The first thing she did was to alert the medical team. She spoke with the nurses and the anesthesiologist. She spoke of Chiara, of her story, of that of her babies. She told them that she had been her patient, but now she was also a friend. She handed Chiara over to them as a precious treasure to guard and to treat with great care. In the cold operating room, she stood close to her, placing her rosary in the palm of her hand and squeezing it. It was the rosary bracelet that Chiara had brought her from Medjugorje.

"All the surgeries were like this," Daniela related. She was near her each time, but always feeling impotent. It was a sign "that I was there as a friend; but, more important, there was also her Mamma [Mary]. Together, we helped each other not to doubt and to trust each other."

In the silence of that room, prayer was the only thing that Chiara was able to perceive. She was awake because the anesthesia was local, but she did not exchange looks with anyone. In fact her eyes were covered in order to protect them from the strong light that the surgery required and that was focused directly on her face.

Fighting fear with faith, Daniela was at the right of Chiara and assisted in everything during the surgery. From her position, she saw the surgeon operate, but she could not see the lesion directly. The expressions of those present, however, spoke eloquently, the anesthesiologist in particular. Daniela heard her murmur: "There is no doubt it is a carcinoma."

The extracted mass was analyzed without delay. According to the immediate examination it was precisely that, a carcinoma. But this exam was considered provisional; to be certain, it would be necessary to wait for the definitive histological exam. The surgeon then decided to make a second cut in order to take other small samples of tissue at the margins of the lesion. These little particles were free and clean.

Meanwhile Daniela tried to hear Francesco. She wished to see whether he was continuing to move in Chiara's belly, if he was okay. She did not hear anything, and for a moment was afraid that something had happened to him. She then tried to calm Chiara, telling her that everything was okay and that Francesco was fine. Chiara interpreted her baby's silence as a delicate collaboration with his mamma. After a bit Francesco began to move again. The anesthesia had had a light effect on him also, but nothing serious.

After the surgery Daniela was again with Chiara, holding her hand in the recovery room.

"I spoke a little, but just a little," Daniela said, "Words were useless. I had only a great desire to cry; I was there, and I tried to pray in silence."

The mass removed from the surgery was greater than expected.

Meanwhile, while she waited outside with Enrico, Chiara's parents arrived. When she left, Daniela saw them and, forcing a smile, told them that the surgery had succeeded without complications and that Chiara would soon return to her room. She cautioned them that is was still necessary to wait for the definitive histological exam. Later she would also repeat these words to Enrico, when at the end of that long day, she would accompany him home in the car. "Is it a tumor?" he asked.

"I said neither yes nor no," Daniela related, "because I could not lie."

After the surgery, Chiara was not able to speak, and she had enormous difficulty swallowing. Therefore, eating was completely excluded. Expressing herself with her eyes and writing on a piece of paper, she tried to convince the nurses to give her something stronger than the Tylenol that they had prescribed for her. The pains to her tongue were truly intense, lacerating. However, because of her pregnant condition, the hospital personnel refused to give her more powerful pain killers. She asked only that God help her. She passed a terrible night.

Recalling those hours, she would write: "Without being able to speak and not being able to swallow saliva, I lived the longest night of my life. While crying silently, I said to God: 'Why don't You help me? I know that You can do it!' At a certain point, nearly delirious, I said: 'God does not exist; otherwise He would not do this to me.' But at that moment I felt a strong pain in my heart, and I felt very much alone, as alone as I had ever been; and I was saddened for having had such a thought."

At a certain point, after having said these words, Chiara felt another pain, an even more profound suffering, that of the one who felt abandoned on the Cross: the sorrow of Jesus. It was a test of faith. Nearly a year later, when she will feel her Spouse coming for her, it would be this night that would rekindle fear in her heart. She would fear not the pain of suffering in itself but the doubt that she had been capable of insinuating, for having vacillated in her faith, in her trust in God. Her Lord is a good Father who sent His Son to die for love; and she had not ever been capable of believing the contrary. (For Chiara it would be the only trial of this type.)

In the morning, when Enrico arrived, she had just fallen asleep.

"When I awoke," she related, "Enrico was next to me, reading the *Fonti Francescani*." Her eyes opened precisely while her husband was proclaiming the extraordinary words of St. Francis on perfect joy: the discovery of God's will in adversity, of a love that confronts pain and that knows how to transform evil into good. To Chiara it seemed true. She immediately thought that, even if during that night she had not understood anything and had denounced Him, God had not abandoned her. For her it was marvelous to see how God continued to love her through the person He put next to her. Her dolorous "experience that challenged her faith,"[11] and the spiritual dryness lived in the preceding hours, were finished.

Chiara immediately made her husband understand that she wished to sign out of the hospital. To remain seemed useless. Once out, Daniela prescribed more effective anti-pain pills. This helped her very much. Chiara remained grateful to Daniela for a long time for this enormously compassionate gesture.

After she went home, communicating was difficult. Chiara suffered much and was not able to speak. The Sunday following the surgery, she and Enrico went to Mass in the parish of Santa Francesca Romana. Arm in arm with her husband, who spoke for her, interpreting her gestures and intentions, Chiara smiled, although with her mouth closed.

For the first time, she appeared challenged and in low spirits. But she mustered her spirits and went forward. All this makes

---

[11] Semen, *The Spiritualità coniugale secondo Giovanni Paolo II*, 79.

sense "if only for Francesco," she wrote in her diary, who being so little and defenseless has "had to confront emotions and fears so great."

The result of the definitive histological exam arrived. It read as follows: *Squamous Cell Carcinoma poorly differentiated, (G3); infiltrating the body of the tongue due to cohesive (massive) invasion. It displays perineural infiltration and vascular vessel invasion, staging* pT1.

It was the identification card of a monster: *squamous cell carcinoma* is a scaly, flaky tumor, the most serious, in which the good cells are indistinguishable from the bad. The malignant cells had entered the tongue en masse without leaving any areas healthy. They had also metastasized (transferred) to other areas: the nerve tissue and the blood vessels.

Chiara had never smoked, and she had a carcinoma on her tongue: there was no logical connection. First Maria, then Davide, now Chiara herself: "The Lord humiliates the wise" (cf. 1 Cor. 1:27), Enrico often recalled in his testimonies.

Chiara would call her tumor "the dragon," just as the much-loved Don Tonino Bello had done with the evil that had attacked him. Chiara's final battle would be the battle against the dragon, engaged precisely when—as in a fable—little Francesco finally arrived as recompense after a long struggle.

After some time passed, Chiara's voice returned and she felt better. Little Francesco was growing, and so was her belly.

One evening, we were at dinner at their house, and Cristiana profited from a moment when they were alone in order to be able, finally, to speak to Chiara after so much time. Chiara told her of the operation and of how worried she had been for the life in her womb. She feared the anesthesia or some other thing that might harm him. She spoke to her of Daniela, who pressed the rosary Chiara had given her in her hands.

Francesco and the Dragon

She told Cristiana that she had kept repeating to Daniela, "Dear friend, I am so sorry that you had to see me so butchered. It could not [have been] a beautiful sight!" Even in that occasion she was concerned about the others. She then told Cristiana that at a certain point she did not feel the baby move around. Even during the surgery, Francesco was in her thoughts.

We switched topics and began speaking of our weddings, of the preparations and of the wedding gowns. Chiara said that on the day of her wedding, she found true happiness. She had given herself totally, and all that mattered to her was [for her and Enrico] to embrace together whatever God was proposing to them, day by day.

How was she living the illness? "The illness prostrates you; it knocks you down physically. But the uncertainties during the engagement, the fear of losing Enrico—that was truly a suffering that I no longer live. I will never ever turn back. Much better the illness. To be finally one with Enrico makes everything livable. Nothing can be compared with all the anxiety [I] experienced before the marriage."

Now she was happy to do everything possible for her baby. She wished to place him first, before all her needs, to do what a mamma must do during nine months of pregnancy, in order to give him the possibility of being born. This is what interested Chiara.

At this point, in order to understand the best way to go, she began, along with the monthly post-operative visits, some parallel activities: a series of medical appointments and consultations with specialists and oncologists. The operation that she had just undergone was only the first phase of the total surgery she required. Remaining were the lymph nodes on her neck that needed emptying and might contain tumoral cells.

Husband and wife, young and smiling, faced each day with serenity. Just a few hours after the surgeon's definitive words, Chiara invited Daniela to dinner. "Today, we are having fish!" she told her—she who could eat solely pureed food.

In a short time Daniela was able to obtain an appointment at the Tumor Institute of Milan. Enrico and Chiara departed Rome on March 28, accompanied by their friend Angelo, a geriatrician. They had met him and his family after Davide Giovanni's funeral. Chiara was particularly grateful for the friendships that the Lord sent their way during the course of this story. The friendship with Angelo and his wife, Elisa, was one of these friendships. Elisa would also serve as the wet nurse for the newborn Francesco when Chiara was unable to feed him.

At Milan the specialists gave their opinion. They knew Chiara's story, that twice she had refused to abort. Therefore, the interruption of this pregnancy, usually considered an option in cases like these, was immediately discarded.

Therefore, it would be possible to proceed with the second phase of the surgery only after the birth of Francesco. However, according to the doctors, waiting for the natural date of birth would very much compromise the efficacy of the cure. They preferred to anticipate the birth by a few weeks and induce labor just after the baby had reached pulmonary maturity.

The first proposal was optimal in terms of cures for the mother, but the most aggressive for the baby. Chiara would have been able to have her tongue wound reevaluated and her lymph nodes cleaned in standard time, which is within forty-five days of the first operation. Inducing labor, in case of the positivity of the tumoral cells, would enable the mamma to undergo radiotherapy and chemotherapy. As for the newborn, he would have to live in an incubator for the first few weeks of his life. The surgeon would be able to conclude his work, but the baby's survival would be at risk. Chiara excluded this possibility.

The doctors advised waiting even up to sixty days after the surgery, fifteen more than customary, but absolutely not beyond; this would require that Francesco be born at thirty-four weeks. Even in this case, the baby would be in an incubator. The doctors proposed having the birth as soon as possible. Enrico's anxiety tore at him; he wanted his son to have a mother, and he wanted to have his son. Chiara desired a cure (indeed, she had submitted to the first operation solely with the help of local anesthesia) but not at the expense of the baby, for whom she intended to postpone the second part of the cures in order not to put him at risk. After the birth of Francesco, she would accept every type of treatment, even the most invasive.

"To a majority of the doctors," Chiara wrote, "Francesco is a seventh-month fetus. And the one who should be saved is me. But I have no intention of putting the life of Francesco at risk for some uncertain statistics that are supposed to make me believe that I should allow my baby to be born premature so that the surgeons can operate on me."

"The difficult decision," she continued, "was to understand how to attack this tumor as soon as possible without putting the life of Francesco in peril." Chiara did not wish to risk the life of Francesco in order to save her own. It was not enough for her that the dangers to the baby were reduced; she desired that there were none at all. She wished to be certain that she had done everything that she, as a mother, was able to do for him at this moment. Francesco had to be born healthy and at the opportune moment; otherwise Chiara was not with them.

Unfortunately, some of the doctors did not seem to understand the gravity of her concern, nor did they share the reasons for it. To Chiara it seemed that they were still looking to save only her, without taking into account that there was another life in play. It irritated her that some specialists were willing to put at risk her son's life. Chiara did not at all think that this creature was depriving her of something that belonged to her, that he was coming into the world in order to kill her, that he was her enemy. Rather, she thought of herself as something that already belonged to Francesco, and she wished to be certain that, throughout his last very precious months inside her, she was giving her all to him. "Another day, another thirty-eight grams more before the birth of the baby," she would repeat to the doctors, seeking to ensure the complete formation of the baby.

Chiara wanted to wait. To wait until Francesco was able to live without the incubator. It concerned only five or six days, at the most, falling precisely at the thirty-fourth week, on May 15. If the baby had to risk something, they must be natural risks related to the birth.

Chiara knew that little by little Francesco was growing in her womb and that together with him the dragon was also growing. But as a mother, she wished to assume those risks that were hanging over her baby, relieving him of this weight by taking it upon herself. Going forward with the weeks, waiting as much as possible, would set the risk for him at zero. It was simply love. Her only thought was that of giving Francesco everything he needed. This is what Chiara wished to do: to go as far as she was able. So for her—notwithstanding the availability of the doctors—the visit was a disappointment.

(The most beautiful part of that day, Chiara would tell us, was seeing the Duomo of Milan.)

It irritated her that they kept referring to the baby as a fetus, even though she kept repeating that his name is Francesco. The only thing she could do at that moment [and she was determined] was to let him develop and become as strong as possible.

"I was agitated. I felt an ugly sensation. I did not know who took my side and who was trying to dissuade me: including Enrico. I felt like a lioness who was trying to defend her cub. I felt an aggressiveness I had never experienced before. After I got home, I said to Enrico: 'Whose side are you taking? I have not changed my mind.'"

We had never heard Chiara speak like this: terrible, as the Bible says, was that beauty and fearful strength. But then Chiara understood that her husband wanted solely to take care of her. Even he was ready to gamble everything. Enrico explained it like this: "It is as if you must choose between having your furniture stolen or your house demolished." For the first time it was not a child at risk, but one of the two [of them] who could die.

From that moment Chiara, helped also by the events and by the persons close to her, put into action a special strategy. She began with seeking the counsel of the doctors who valued Francesco's needs. Like Jesus during the trial, she saw the involvement of all—the Sanhedrin, Herod, and Pilate—and she proceeded with her Passion, seeming to submit to events that in reality, like Jesus, she was leading. Chiara began to make monthly clinical appointments for the lymph nodes on her neck and the lesions on her tongue. Given that, at the end of March, the X-rays did not show any traces of the lesions, and having had some additional treatments, she reached a compromise with the specialists to wait a little longer than foreseen in order to permit Francesco to reach thirty-five or thirty-six weeks.

"However, this decision distressed me so much. I did not at all wish to leave my son in an incubator without being able to go see him because I was confined in another department in order to have surgery. But Daniela assured me that she would do everything possible to have the baby placed with me in the same room. She said that many babies at thirty-six weeks have no need of the incubator." In the end, Chiara accepted it.

She continued to submit to examinations, and in the meantime she prayed. She prayed to thank God for these last two weeks granted to Francesco's development. She prayed that during this time, in which each day represented a victory for her and for Francesco, the will of the Father would be done. She prayed that, one way or another, she could postpone the surgery for a few more days, for the good of Francesco. Father Vito, in relating these episodes, said rightly that "Chiara did not die because of Francesco; she gave her life for Francesco."

In those days husband and wife were drawn to Assisi. They wished to thank God for the way in which He was leading them. As always they looked inward for their support, for their trust in God. But at the same time, the umpteenth battle for understanding their situation was bursting out all around them. Enrico explained how they continued to fight the spiritual battles, ever searching within for the understanding of that faith in God that was, as always, their only comfort. "Maria Grazia Letizia was a daughter of God," Enrico explained. "We did not need to understand whose child she was; it was those around us who at all costs wished to understand. And it was the same for Davide and for Chiara; God has used a very special pedagogy."

Yes, He did, because God, Enrico continued to relate, chose pathologies for his children and for his wife that had nothing to do with each other; they were rare and independent. First was the anencephaly of Maria Grazia Letizia, which had led to the idea that the next child would have the same problem; but then there were the malformations of Davide Giovanni that were completely diverse.

Finally there was the tumor on Chiara's tongue, the most unusual occurrence for a young woman. "It is precisely God who gives you a sign," continued Enrico, whose interpretation of the health of Francesco upset the superficial faith of many who call themselves believers: " 'I am maintaining my promise,' God told us. 'You have understood that in Maria and in Davide I also was there; it is true. Now there is Francesco, your son, and he is healthy. There is no correlation. It is I who created Maria Grazia Letizia like this; I created Davide Giovanni like this, and I created Francesco as he is. And it is I who created Chiara's tumor.' We are angry with God because we know that He is behind everything, but at the same time, to understand that God is behind everything is wonderful."

The Petrillos' rapport with God was never so authentic. They knew that they were involved in a decisive way and not only for themselves. God was asking them to become His disciples. The spirit of Chiara welcomed the invitation, but there were still more steps to take.

Meanwhile Enrico and Chiara continued to entrust themselves to Jesus. They knew that He wished them well, and even if they did not understand, they remained serene. In the Petrillo home, there was a little tradition of making a spiritual retreat before each birth. This time Enrico and Chiara chose the monastery of the Clares of San Girolamo (St. Jerome) at Gubbio. The nuns were quite taken by them. When they heard them chanting and singing their prayers, they would interrupt their activity to listen to it.

Chiara wrote in her notes: "In my heart, I continued to ask God to allow me to carry on my role as a mamma in the best possible way. I knew that I was protecting him while he was in my belly. Then, [when he was born], I would nurse him, giving him love together with antibodies. These were the things for which there was no substitute, and I wished to give them to my son."

With each small step Chiara accepted and guarded the Word of God: she knew she would not be able to find the strengths that she needed solely in herself, and she remained constantly open to a word that could transform the life of her and Enrico. Often one little verse that God suggested was enough for her. When they had discovered that their children were ready for heaven, it was the Word that permitted the young couple to confront the journey and to see life in death: only one word, like that of the Archangel Gabriel to Mary.

Chiara wrote in her notes what the Lord was "saying" to them during the pregnancy with Francesco, and this time the words, episodes really, were two, but the two corresponded strongly one with the other. The first was the Jewish Feast of Booths or Tabernacles. When His people arrived in the Promised Land, God asked that they remember their origins; that they keep in their minds and in their hearts all that had been given to them, and that their [true] country was in Heaven. Chiara wrote: "The Lord does not wish us to put down roots."

The other episode is that of the disciples at Emmaus, who after the Resurrection recognized Christ in the breaking of the bread. "In the beginning," Chiara wrote, "we did not recognize Him in the tumor."

The date of the birth, postponed from May 15 to May 23, was delayed again, thanks to a providential congress that engaged the surgeon scheduled for the surgery. To Chiara's joy, everything was put off for another week. Her prayer had been heard. She waited as long as she could to protect Francesco. "Perhaps the reason I have Francesco today," Enrico reflected, "is because of this, her choice. If we had chosen differently, no one would be able to convince me that our son would be here with me."

During those days, Chiara spoke only of the baby; she coddled him, caressing her belly. One evening when we were together, Chiara took Cristiana aside and asked her if she would like to make a memorial of their story, creating and writing a fable for Francesco. She wished him to know and to remember his two siblings in Heaven. "He has these two enormous gifts next to him, and I want him to know them well. And who better to tell him their story than you and Simone?"

This time also she did not wish to be the one to decide the day of the little one's birth. They joked about the fact that she and Enrico could not bring themselves to buy anything for him. They could not even begin to think that he would be remaining with them. Smiling, Enrico would say, "Wait, Chia', let's not waste euro!" They always made us laugh so much. They could not believe their happiness.

However, Francesco received many little outfits as gifts. During the days before the birth, Chiara, filled with emotion and anticipation, passed the time folding and arranging them as if she were preparing herself better for the great event. Meanwhile Enrico completed some big projects in the house to make it more welcoming for the little one.

On May 30, at 6:30 in the morning, Chiara and Enrico waited for Daniela in front of her house. It was the day scheduled for Francesco's birth, and the threesome was going together to the Fatebenefratelli Hospital. After they arrived, both husband and wife went to Mass in the hospital's church. Daniela left them saying: "I shall think of the things down here, and you can think of the things up there."

In a little less than an hour, Daniela returned to call them. It was time to go up to the room. When they arrived, Enrico and Chiara prayed the Office, and Daniela joined them. How strange, she was thinking, looking around. It was the place she had gone nearly every day to work, and now she was there praying. But with those two, so many strange things become natural.

Francesco was born at thirty-seven weeks, just a couple of weeks before the end of the pregnancy. The birth was spontaneous and without complications. The baby was beautiful, and Enrico and Chiara were happy. When they were no longer holding him in their arms, they contemplated him sleeping in the cradle, in ecstasy.

Chiara wrote:

> The birth was slow, calm, and extremely sweet. In the delivery room there was a very tranquil atmosphere. With me there were Enrico, Daniela, and the obstetrician.... Then, within the space of a few pushes, a little dark-skinned "urchin" came into the world and, attaching himself to me, began to suckle. This was the great gift I had to renounce with Maria and Davide. I was so happy to be able to give him what all mammas in nature give to their own children to make them strong.
>
> I knew that my role at that moment was simply that; I did not have to do anything more or anything less; only to reassure him, nurse him, and prepare him for his encounter with the external world.... I had feared that after the surgery I would not have had the strength to hold Francesco and that he would feel abandoned; he who was so sensible and so needy of physical contact. That evening, in silence, Enrico and I cried together. We never

ever wished to be separated, and ... we did not know what we were going to meet.

Chiara needed another operation for the cleaning of the lymph nodes. The surgical procedure initiated in March had to be concluded as soon as possible. Perhaps she would be able to nurse Francesco immediately after the operation. It could not be excluded.

Anyhow, she had already asked Elisa, Angelo's wife, and Lucia, another friend who had recently given birth, to substitute for her in this task if it were necessary. She told them that it would make her very happy.

For Elisa and Lucia, it was a moving request. Chiara's renunciation was extraordinary: How many mammas would have done the same? How many would have chosen to hand over this privilege even in a situation that was more than legitimate? For the good of her own son, she chose to have someone else assure him that spontaneity and simplicity that she knew she could not personally guarantee during the days following his birth. Chiara was willing to go as far as she was able for the good of Francesco and in this, she succeeded.

For the two women, the situation was a bit strange. Finding themselves nursing someone else's child was also a little embarrassing. But the next day, when Chiara asked to be with them during the nursing so that Francesco, still hungry, would sleep serenely, the shame immediately vanished. The joy emanating from Chiara's face when she saw him eating satisfied and the simplicity with which she called them "Francesco's wet nurses" dissipated all their concerns.

Chiara had completely accepted the limits of her body that had placed her at a crossroads. If the choice had been put before her of curing herself or of bringing her baby into the world at his own pace, her body, instead of pushing against her, would have held her to giving herself. Chiara understood that the only way to love was to be yourself. She accepted her body even at that moment, with its incapacity to feed Francesco.

Two days before the operation, the evening of June 1, Chiara was silent. Preoccupying her—and frightening her—was the discussion with the surgeon about the risks and the possible successes and outcomes of the operation. When Lucia arrived at the hospital, she found Chiara seated on the bed, lights off, with Francesco in her arms. The doctor had spoken of spasms at her shoulder and of a possible tracheotomy. While Enrico was out, Chiara opened her mouth solely to ask Lucia to nurse Francesco, and she handed him over to her. She lay down, but she was not able to sleep or even to rest. The silence was broken only by the hunger of the little one.

On June 3, Chiara had surgery, sixty-nine days after the first operation. It was imperative to proceed. Besides cleaning the lymph nodes, it was also necessary to examine the wound on her tongue. So, early in the morning, accompanied by Enrico, she exited the gynecological area holding Francesco. A little later a nurse delicately took the little one from her and brought him to the pediatric ward. Chiara cried. Separating herself from her baby was a true sorrow. She and Enrico looked at each other and with that glance said good-bye. Daniela also assisted at this compassionate moment, and then she turned toward the operating room to help prepare Chiara for the surgery.

Her friend Elisa, also present at this scene, accompanied her to the surgical floor. Chiara now and then smiled from under the sheet. Elisa, having been taken for her sister (they shared the same name), was able to remain with her until the moment she entered the operating room. After she left Chiara, she stayed around to pray and to wait.

Then, going out on the bank of the Tiber, Enrico and Elisa read that day's Gospel. It seemed to speak precisely of Chiara.

In truth I tell you, you will be weeping and wailing while the world will rejoice; you will be sorrowful, but your sorrow will turn into joy. A woman in childbirth suffers, because her time has come; but when she has given birth to the child forgets the suffering in her joy that a human being has been born into the world. So it is with you: you are sad now, but I will see you again, and your hearts will be full of joy, and joy no one shall take from you. When that day comes you will not ask me any questions. (John 16:20–23)

It is a Gospel that consoles and that instills strength. To Enrico it immediately brought to mind the Morning Prayer of that same day: "I will turn their mourning into joy, I will comfort them, and give them gladness for sorrow" (Jer. 31:13). Instinctively he thought that his wife would recover, that after the operation everything would conclude for the better, as one could humanly imagine it. But that word *mourning* suggested to his heart the more profound truth, which at that moment he could not recognize, but which would remain in the memory of his heart.

A little later, Chiara's parents also joined them. All together they entered the hospital and went to the chapel to pray. The wait was difficult. Keeping them informed were messages from Daniela, who again was next to her friend in the operating room, rosary in hand as always. Her words gave them hope. The first good news was about Chiara's tongue; it was clean.

Then another group of visitors joined them, among them Elisa, Chiara's sister. They continued to pray, this time outside the hospital on a bench. Several hours passed before Daniela announced the extemporaneous results of the biopsy: the lymph nodes had no trace of the disease. The exam was made on only one part of the lymph nodes, but it was already a lot. Everyone was emotional (if the results were confirmed, it would truly change the prognosis: Chiara would also be able to avoid chemotherapy and radiation therapy). At the end of the procedure, Daniela remained next to her friend and waited for her to revive.

The group [of visitors] hurried to the surgery department. They all wished to see Chiara and to hear what the surgeon had to say following the operation. The news of the negative lymph nodes made them happy, but they found Chiara awake and suffering. Not one among those present was prepared for that vision.

"Semi-awake and with a bandage covering her neck, Chiara was swollen from the new cut on her tongue and no part of her body was without pain," her friend Elisa related. She was immobilized in her bed; the cut on her neck impeded her from moving or speaking. Her breasts were swollen, hardened from the milk that had appeared on that day and that Francesco had not suckled in the last few hours, during the surgery. Furthermore, she had lost blood from the baby's delivery, just two days before.

To everyone—Enrico, Chiara's parents, her sister, and all the friends gathered around her—it appeared that they were before the martyred body of Jesus the evening of Good Friday. No one could have foreseen or understood what the surgery would involve or how difficult and delicate the convalescence would be—not even Chiara, who, upon awakening, became aware that the overhaul of her tongue had touched more than she could have ever thought. "Controlling the margins" was now translated into an extirpation that impeded the tongue from reaching her front teeth. Chiara was very ill.

The surgeon who had operated on her was content with how the surgery had gone, but he said that it was necessary to wait for the definitive histological results. The future course would depend on these. The fact that the extemporaneous exam was negative left them with hope.

During that sorrowful afternoon, Chiara was not able to smile, nor did she have any wish to speak. She asked for no one.

The following morning, we went to the hospital. Chiara was gloomy and still teary: she was on her side, bandaged, swollen, and attached to drainage. Through Enrico we learned that she was very angry and uncomfortable. She had not known that with the operation they would alter her tongue again. Everything made her angry, and it was distressing to see her like this. Cristiana was caressing her leg, and she was crying. She could not bear to see the contented faces around her. We looked at each other in silence.

Enrico was anxious for his wife but very happy about Francesco. He brought the baby so we could see him. He was already beautiful. The next day Chiara was a little better. We brought her frappes. Enrico suggested the flavors. Only he knew how to interpret his wife's grunts and grimaces. Anyhow, to us they were a beautiful couple. United in this trial, their love was once again augmented, raised up to another level.

* * *

The days immediately following the operation were very difficult. Helping Chiara was a challenge. No one was prepared to do it well. Francesco seemed to succeed better than anyone else. That same Sunday, Chiara, in a wheelchair, went to find him in the pediatric department. The morphine she was taking was not a high dosage, so she was permitted to nurse him. The news made her extremely happy. Even the pain was more bearable.

Father Vito said that a body like that of Chiara, like that of Jesus, wounded, pierced, and bleeding, makes us see that one lives not because one breathes, but because one loves. Life makes sense only when it is consumed for another. Chiara's fruitfulness was marvelous; for her, to die was truly to live.

On June 7, Chiara left the hospital together with Enrico and Francesco. She was emotional and content. She said that now she and her husband finally would try to be full-time parents. It was the first time that they left the hospital ward with a child in their arms.

In that period they lived something that nearly approached the daily reality of a normal family. For the first time, Chiara was at home fussing with a little baby. Now, like all parents, they could join the discussions of the baby's little disturbances; of her and Enrico's first sleepless nights, and of their first excursions as a threesome. During one of these, they took Francesco to visit his sister and brother at the cemetery.

Then, on June 15, the definitive results of the histological exam arrived. Two of the sixteen lymph nodes examined were positive, touched by the disease, revealing not only signs of the malignity but also the strong aggressivity of the tumor. Those few infected cells had succeeded in piercing the wall of the lymph nodes.

It was Daniela and Massimiliano who told this to Chiara. It was late Thursday evening. They drank a tisane together, and then the two friends asked Enrico to bring the guitar and to sing a song. He chose one dedicated to the Virgin Mary. After the song ended, they gave them the news. Chiara would have to begin chemotherapy and radiation therapy, for which she would naturally have to suspend nursing. The Petrillos remained smiling and calm.

It was a very difficult summer, but they faced it trusting totally in God and in His plans.

Chiara nursed Francesco nearly to the end of the month, and then, on June 29, she went to Foligno for the PET TAC (an imaging test that looks for disease in the body). The exam would complete the clinical picture. That day, she was not able to see the baby. As far as it seemed, there was no metastasis in the interval. Chiara had to begin the treatments, but first a little tube would have to be put in her for alimentation, because the inflammation caused by some of the treatment would compromise her ability to swallow, preventing her from eating normally. In reality, at a certain point, the ulcers in her mouth would also impede her from drinking; because through the ulcers, the water would pass from the esophagus to the trachea and arrive at the lungs, provoking a powerful pneumonia.

On the day scheduled for the insertion of the tube, July 13, Chiara was unable to go. A few days before, Francesco had had a high fever and he was still recovering. It did not concern anything particularly serious, so everything was resolved in a few days.

During that time, we were at Rome and the Petrillos had told us of Francesco's fever and recovery. Chiara invited us to join them at the home of her parents in order to spend a little time together. She was really down. The separation from her son did not please her, and neither did the fact that the baby would also have to live this experience. She was sad and could not wait to go to him and nurse him again. She was still bandaged.

When we visited her again, it was at the hospital. Chiara was able once more to feed Francesco but when she had to say good night to him, her eyes filled with tears. It displeased her that the little one was crying and that the nurse had taken him from her arms and was carrying him away. During supper together she was telling us that she had such a desire for normalcy, of going around the stalls at the open market ... the usual activities. She also said that evidently for them it was not possible.

Chiara had the tube inserted during the second half of July. She had to take in food through her stomach with a large syringe. For her it became nearly automatic. At the table, the food was blessed and then they began to eat; Enrico and the frequent guests eating normally and Chiara injecting something of substance through the syringe. After a while, however, she renounced this system and instead applied a sack with nutrition in the evening. Each day she said her "Here I am" to God.

On August 1, she began her daily treatments at the day hospital: the radiotherapy on her neck, five days a week and the chemotherapy every twenty-one days. Chiara began the treatment at Rome in order to give Francesco the love and presence that he needed. [The doctors had also considered the therapies at New York, Baltimore, and Monaco, but in the end they endorsed the radiotherapy done at Rome.]

During the first days, the nausea was incredible. She joked, saying that now she knew how other pregnant women felt. During her three pregnancies, she had never vomited.

She and Enrico decided to move in temporarily with Chiara's parents in their house in the country. They said they would be much better off there, because they had more privacy; there was much more space, and it favored a life in common [with all the family]. The grandparents helped them much with Francesco. It was there that Chiara and Enrico had spent the very first weeks of their marriage.

The treatments would take the entire summer and half of September.

In this period, Chiara grew very thin, something for which the oncologists scolded her. Her nose was so dry that it required her to humidify the entire house, not just the room where she slept. Her voice became increasingly weaker, so much so that it became very difficult for her to speak at all. As after the first surgery; she became aphonic (voiceless) for a certain period. Then, when she was able to speak again, she preferred to remain silent; as if, her father recalled, that difficult experience, lived with such serenity, had taught her to overcome the apparent need to intervene in a discussion.

The treatments were painful. It was a difficult trial, and the many collateral effects (among them, vomiting and bleeding skin) exhausted her. Yet during these treatments Chiara listened to songs written and played by her husband on her MiCorder mp3. Up until the vigil of Francesco's birth, she herself had accompanied these same pieces live with her violin. House on the Rock was the group in which Enrico played, together with some friends. Beautiful and smiling, she was there with them listening to the story of her and Enrico in the music.

In addition to Enrico, her son gave her much consolation. In spite of her tiredness, she held him in her arms and tenderly caressed him as much as possible.

Even if by September the heaviest therapies were finished, Chiara was not able to take up her former life immediately. Indeed, initially her immune defenses were still very low, so her isolation continued. Moreover, she had not yet recouped her voice. Despite all this, she was always affectionate with everyone.

The love of so many friends and persons close to her during these difficult times astonished her.

Beginning in October, things began to go better, and Chiara was able to take up a nearly regular routine. She gradually regained her voice and, slowly, began to drink and eat. The previous January she had taken on a job at Acli (the Italian Christian Workers Association already mentioned) but then had had to interrupt her employment for the pregnancy. Now that she was better, she wished to take it up again, finishing what she had begun. Chiara had a fear of leaving things halfway. (As a mother, she had wished to choose a profession that permitted her to spend as much time as possible with her children.)

Then, when the [results of] the first tests said that everything was okay, Chiara set out once more to have a somewhat normal life. Like her husband, she also worked half a day. Both were able to be very present with Francesco. It was a beautiful period, and they were serene, even if the therapies had left her physically weak and bruised.

Liberated from the feeding tube—she had done everything to free herself from it—she was still unable to eat as before. The radiotherapy had caused her to lose salivation nearly completely, and this required her to drink often. In order to send down just a little bite she had to resort to drinking a glass and a half of water. Further, at night, she would wake up with the sensation that she could not breathe.

* * *

Providence had arranged that by September we would be at Rome each week. We were extremely happy to see each other so often, and Cristiana would meet Chiara nearly each afternoon. It was a very beautiful period, a simple daily routine. There were hard moments also, but at the same time they were lightened by a joy that transformed everything.

Chiara's confidence was steadily increasing. She was delighted that Francesco was so good with Cristiana, since he found it difficult to be with anyone who was not his mamma or his papà.

She and Enrico had enrolled in a catechism course created by Father Fabio Rosini, and they were very enthusiastic; it seemed to lighten and unburden them. Chiara spoke of how much it was helping them to clarify their situation. The afternoons were tranquilly spent, and Francesco was always serene. While Cristiana accompanied him outside for walks, Chiara profited from the time to take a shower and to sleep. Joking, she would say that she was happy to have seen her son's first crush; with Cristiana he would laugh and play joyfully.

Chiara often said that Francesco had need for normalcy. He had already lived too many emotions, and he could use a little calm, even if it were at the expense of his mamma. Once she recalled having said to God, "During the first nine months the mamma is indispensable; and for the first months after birth she is fundamental; and for the first ten years [she is] important. I hope that I can be there until then, but meanwhile help me to do my best today." Everyone was speechless over her openness. Chiara always had so many concerns, but she easily forgot about herself.

Shortly after the end of the treatment, the doctors had to evaluate the effects of the therapy. The first TAC, of November 18, revealed some lesions on the lungs that were very diffuse. The clinical picture was surprising for the precocity and the speed with which these new lesions were established. In the previous PET exam, taken just four and a half months before, nothing so dramatic had emerged. At that point Chiara was bombarded with cures and subjected to a rather heavy cycle of chemotherapy. In light of all that, it was expected that the therapy would cause the devastation, indeed, even the blocking of the tumoral development. However, it did not at all function like this. Indeed, it weakened Chiara's already precarious immune defenses, to the point of causing an increase in the lesions and provoking in her already run-down condition what initially seemed to be an interstitial pneumonia—that is, a pneumonia situated between the cells of other tissues. But then, when treatments for various pneumonias were applied, this one did not go away.

No one could have known that under the inflammation, in hiding and fearlessly advancing, was the dragon (the cancer). In order to eliminate any doubt, it was necessary to take more tests, in January.

On December 16, little Francesco was baptized. The godparents were Daniela and Massimiliano, who then added Juan Diego to the baby's name. The celebration was held in the Church of Our Lady of Guadalupe, Enrico and Chiara's neighborhood parish on Via Aurelia. On that day, Francesco had a bit of a fever and, not being able to celebrate with his parents and friends, was looked after by his grandparents. Chiara was very content that her son had received this grace. Also they, like Juan Diego, had discovered that they could entrust themselves to a Mother ever ready to sustain them with her presence.

During the homily, Father Vito spoke of the Gospel that relates the slaughter of the innocents. Just as, in the story of salvation, the innocents had served the mission of Jesus in permitting him to grow, so Maria Grazia Letizia and Davide Giovanni had prepared the path for the littlest brother, who was called to complete a marvelous plan.

Francesco and the Dragon

On her part, Chiara was gradually preparing Francesco for the separation. By renouncing possession of him and the idea that he belonged to her, she was truly demonstrating her love for him. She knew that she had to slacken her hold on him. The Lord had a greater gift ready for her.

For this reason, she would more often have her husband hold him in his arms and try to content him. She also gave up nursing Francesco so that he would learn to do with less of her presence.

At the end of the month of January 2012, there was a new PET TAC. The result seemed good; it seemed that there was no metastasis to the lungs. But in a following consultation, the lung specialist told Angelo that he would advise a bronchoscopy (for an internal inspection of the lungs). Chiara, however, was not able to confront this type of exam. She was too tired. So they decided to have only a test for pneumonia, and then they would choose the suitable antibiotics on the basis of the results. Everything was checked: the possibility of fungus, tuberculosis, or anything that may have resulted from the lowering of the immune defenses following the treatments. Then Chiara began the antibiotics.

In the months following, from mid-February on, she continued to lose weight. Then she began to have back pains. At the same time, her mouth began to bleed.

She was not too preoccupied with her back. She joked that being old already, she hoped that things would improve with time. The truth was that, often, the pains were so strong she was unable to hold Francesco; or they would keep her immobilized in her bed.

Cristiana, alternating with other friends, helped her with the little one. Once, when she was not able to move from the bed, she vented with her on the telephone: "I want a normal life. It is my dream. Vito told me that I must give it up, but I find it difficult. Perhaps we have gotten ourselves stuck precisely on this idea, and we have gone awry longing for that blessed normality. I would like to be self-sufficient like everyone; instead I cannot even manage to hold my son in my arms. But why is this my path? Vito has told me that I am still in the phase in which Job is scratching himself with the pottery [see Job 2]. Truly, I am not getting angry again with God. But I am asking Him: what more must I do?"

One morning when Cristiana was at the Petrillos' home, she saw Enrico come out of the bathroom looking worried. He had become aware that his wife was coughing up blood and that it had been going on for some time. The news that it was only the result of a nonthreatening bout with pneumonia was consoling, but it did not eliminate the difficulty and the doubts. Chiara continued to slim down. Her cough was provoked by a reflux (a reverse flow of gastric fluid into the esophagus from the stomach) or by her inability to swallow normally.

In addition, Francesco was having some nocturnal crises. And so, at times, Cristiana would accompany Chiara to the pediatrician. Chiara called her their au pair.

One time, in particular, it was even comical: Chiara had entered the pediatrician's office alone, then introduced him to Cristiana and Francesco, who, while being held was holding a rosary in his hands (one belonging to Cristiana, with which he amused himself). The doctor, knowing Chiara's situation and seeing a baby so little praying the Rosary, literally turned pale. Then the miscomprehension passed, and everyone laughed.

On March 21, it was already time for another exam, a new TAC of the lungs. Afterward, Chiara was feeling well and she decided to take a vacation for a few days with her husband and

Francesco and the Dragon

Francesco; they had much need of it. They were splendid, serene days. She was very happy, even sparkling. She said she had not been so well in an age. It was their first vacation in a long time. They went to Assisi, to Porto Recanati, and then, on the return, they stopped again at Assisi, where some of their friends from Rome joined them and where we were also.

It was March 25, the feast of the Annunciation. Chiara and Enrico entrusted their little one to the hands of Mary in Portiuncula. The Gospel that day invited us to be prepared to lose our life in order to find eternal life.

We dined all together. The table was carefree and full of cheer. After the meal, Chiara felt tired. She found it difficult to walk, and the pain in her back was increasing. She was having difficulty breathing, and she was coughing more.

The next morning we found her at Portiuncula, alone and holding Francesco. She told Cristiana that she had to do something. Although she had slept much, she felt very tired.

When she returned home, the situation did not improve. Waiting for her the next day, March 27, were the results of the TAC.

During an hour in the reception area before the oncological visit, Daniela, who had accompanied them, recalled Enrico saying often: "It is thanks to you, friends, that we are making it."

The results showed evidence of a worsening of the lesions on the lungs. Even more disheartening was the fact that it showed something at the top of the liver; in this case, a number of lesions of some centimeters in diameter.

Barely a week later, on March 28, Chiara submitted to a total-body TAC as a means for comparison. The oncologist requested the close-range exam in order to verify what exactly was going on with those lesions on the liver. The results left everyone speechless.

The TAC revealed some hepatic lesions compatible with the metastasis and a local relapse on the neck. Chiara had been aware for a while of having something on her breast, and during the TAC she also spoke to the radiologist of the pain she was experiencing at her temple. Now her sensations had a correspondence in the exam, which revealed the suspected mammary nodule and an inspissation (thickening) of the right lateral muscle of the right eye. Therefore, not only the lungs but also the eye, the liver, and the breast were infected. The cancer had indeed metastasized. The surprising aggressivity of the tumor, which had worsened the situation in such a brief time, drained away all the doubts. Incredibly, Chiara, once again, was the most disposed to accept it.

When he saw his wife's exam, Enrico instinctively burst into tears. He regretted not being able to keep himself together, but, he would say later, on seeing the images it became evident to him that Chiara had little time left to live.

The next day, Chiara was admitted to the hospital. At Fatebenefratelli the medical team administered an intensive antibiotic therapy that they hoped could be useful. There remained one last hepatic biopsy, which was included to complete the picture of the metastasis.

Chiara was fed up. She could not take any more of hospitals, and after those beautiful days they spent together, the separation from Enrico was too hard. For Cristiana, listening to her speak like this was painful, and the idea of losing her friend cost her much anguish. For Cristiana this was the most difficult part.

However, after a few days, Chiara found her serenity again. Cristiana went to the hospital and immediately found that her friend's room was the one from which the laughs were coming. With her were Daniela and Lucia. Chiara was writing her

memoirs, as Father Vito had asked her to do. "Since I know
that they will be my memoirs, I shall also write the telephone
number of Daniela, so that when you publish them, everyone
will choose her for their doctor. It will be publicity for you!" she
said, smiling. That room with her presence was a marvel. One
left it feeling renewed.

Being away from Enrico weighed very much on Chiara; she
would speak of how great he was with Francesco. When he was
able, he spent time with him on the hospital terrace. He wished
to be with him but not enclosed in a hospital ward. Together
they fed the pigeons the leftover bread from the meal that Chiara
could not manage to eat.

The single room was changed into a triple, and Chiara was in
the middle, next to a nun. It was an arrangement that made her
happy, and she showered the nun with every type of attention.

Meanwhile Enrico, whose fear was always that of being abandoned, lived hours of anguish. He was at home alone with Francesco; and for him also, that week, with Chiara away, was very
difficult—the most terrible week of his life. Living this moment
against his will would also be a preparation. The separation, once
again, strengthened their love.

"That separation was particularly painful," he related. "Not
to be able to console each other, not even with a simple glance
or a simple embrace.... Perhaps because each of us was bringing
the other a little closer to God, not being able to do it, because
you are far from one another, made you suffer so much more."

On March 31, Enrico and Francesco, together with other
families, went to pray at the tomb of John Paul II—a pilgrimage
that Enrico and Chiara had completed alone some days before.

On Sunday, April 1, Chiara wished to go to Mass with her
husband. Granting her request, the nurse simply reminded her that

the only restriction was that she take her antibiotics. When the personnel looked for her, they discovered that she had gone home, taken a shower, and gone to Mass with Enrico. The nurse had simply told her that she could leave the ward, not go away from the hospital! For this misunderstanding Chiara received a reprimand.

During that time, from her room in the middle of the oncological ward, laughs and cheers were heard throughout the area, as if they were coming from another part of the hospital. Chiara did not entertain others with a discourse about herself; it was always about others—Francesco, for example, and his ways. She suffered, but she supported it extremely well.

The hepatic biopsy was scheduled for April 2.

Daniela had seen the tortured body of Chiara many times, her beauty and her serenity intact throughout her trial. In the reception area, she was placed on a stretcher; Daniela stayed with her, standing next to her without speaking.

When they lowered themselves under the machine, they were required to put a little distance between themselves. They were about half a bed length away from one another, but they were able to hold hands, squeezing the rosary. The distance forced Daniela to lean forward. Chiara asked her pardon for the discomfort that the stretching forward caused her.

Daniela could see how thin Chiara was. The exam was done in a high position, a little under the sternum. She was so thin that the needle entered very little. The lance, the tube used in the exam, was nearly all outside her body.

The surgical nurse on duty observed that during the twenty-five years she had worked there, she had never seen a girl so beautiful facing all of this with such a smile.

That evening Chiara would send a message to Daniela, thanking her for having held her hand—a gesture that had made a difference. Before entering the examination room, Daniela, gathering her courage, asked Chiara what she wished her to pray for, imagining that she would have felt like asking for something for herself, in order to face the fear of what would happen. Chiara responded: "Pray for Gaia, because she has not yet accepted her illness." Gaia was a girl who had been ill many years from a tumor, and Chiara had prayed for her from the time she had known her story; she was always in her thoughts. Daniela invariably held this response in her head while she watched her friend breathing with difficulty during the biopsy. With that lance in her chest, she seemed precisely like Jesus on the Cross.

5

September 21: The Wedding

If this book were a film, now would be the moment for a flash-
back. The camera would distance itself from the hospital room
where Chiara was being treated; leave the corridor, the hospital,
the little piazza [out front]; and climb up high, always higher up,
where the roman roofs are seen, the city of Rome, the green,
the mountains of the Apennines, the sea, Italy, and the clouds.
Then it would descend again, going down in a thrashing nose
dive and skim the ground, running and crossing the country
streets and hills.

And now a church is drawing ever closer. We stop before the
façade. We enter. Standing in the central nave is Chiara. She is
dressed as a bride, and next to her is her father. They walk the
short distance to the altar, where Enrico is waiting for her. We
are no longer at Rome on an April day, but at Assisi on a September morning. The church is the splendid Roman cathedral
of San Pietro (St. Peter), and it is filled with guests. It is 2008.

* * *

Assisi was truly an important place for Enrico and Chiara. From
Assisi burst the water that slaked the thirst of the dry earth. It
was here that they listened for the first time to those words that

would accompany them in all their affairs: love is the contrary of possession—a rule that, if it remains firm in the heart, leads to great things, very great things.

The Nuptial Mass

Entrance song, by the bride and groom

My love,
Here you are, finally here,
at the door of my house.
I have been waiting so much time for
this day for us,
serene, I woke up early for you.
Today you shall be mine, my love,
Today you shall be mine, my love.
Come soon, I am waiting here for you,
I still do not believe
you shall give me your hand;
you do not know how much I love you,
I knew also that you were mine.
Today you shall be mine, my love,
Today you shall be mine, my love.
And heaven will open up for us,
love will be born for us
and an angel will sing the love
that God has for us.
Now we are only one in You;
defend this day, our yes, to You.
I shall hold you forever in His heart.
You shall see me forever next to her,
for as long as You wish it.

September 21: The Wedding

Today I shall be yours, my love
Today I shall be yours, my love.
And the heavens will be opened up for us,
love will be born for us,
and an angel will sing the love
that God has for us.
Bells are ringing,
the angels are singing of heaven.

First reading: Isaiah 55:6–9
"Seek the LORD while he may be found,
    call upon him while he is near;
let the wicked forsake his way,
    and the unrighteous man his thoughts;
let him return to the LORD, that he may have mercy
    on him,
    and to our God, for he will abundantly pardon.
For my thoughts are not your thoughts,
    neither are your ways my ways, says the LORD.
For as the heavens are higher than the earth,
    so are my ways higher than your ways
    and my thoughts than your thoughts.

Responsorial psalm: Psalm 128
Song of Ascents
Blessed is every one who fears the LORD,
    who walks in his ways!
You shall eat the fruit of the labor of your hands;
    you shall be happy, and it shall be well with you.

Your wife will be like a fruitful vine
    within your house;

your children will be like olive shoots
   around your table.
Lo, thus shall the man be blessed
   who fears the LORD

THE LORD bless you from Zion!
   May you see the prosperity of Jerusalem
   all the days of your life!
May you see your children's children!
   Peace be upon Israel!

Second reading: Revelation 3:7–13 [emphasis added]
And to the angel of the church in Philadelphia write:

> *The words of the holy one, the true one,*
> *who has the key of David, who opens*
> *and no one shall shut, who shuts and no one opens.*

I know your works. Behold, I have set before you an
open door, which no one is able to shut; I know that you
have but little power, and yet you have kept my word
and have not denied my name. Behold, I will make those
of the synagogue of Satan who say that they are Jews
and are not, but lie—behold, *I will make them come and
bow down before your feet, and learn that I have loved you.*
Because you have kept my word of patient endurance, I
will keep you from the hour of trial which is coming on
the whole world, to try those who dwell upon the earth.
I am coming soon; hold fast what you have, so that no
one may seize your crown. He who conquers, I will make
him a pillar in the temple of my God; never shall he go
out of it, and I will write on him the name of my God,
and the name of the city of my God, the new Jerusalem

which comes down from my God out of heaven, and my own new name. He who has an ear, let him hear what the Spirit says to the churches.

Gospel: Mark 10:17–31

And as he was setting out on his journey, a man ran up and knelt before him, and asked him, "Good Teacher, what must I do to inherit eternal life?" And Jesus said to him, "Why do you call me good? No one is good but God alone. You know the commandments: 'Do not kill, Do not commit adultery, Do not steal, Do not bear false witness, Do not defraud, Honor your father and mother.'" And he said to him, "Teacher, all these I have observed from my youth." And Jesus looking upon him loved him, and said to him, "You lack one thing; go, sell what you have, and give to the poor, and you will have treasure in heaven; and come, follow me." At that saying his countenance fell, and he went away sorrowful; for he had great possessions.

And Jesus looked around and said to his disciples, "How hard it will be for those who have riches to enter the kingdom of God!" And the disciples were amazed at his words. But Jesus said to them again, "Children, how hard it is for those who trust in riches to enter the kingdom of God! It is easier for a camel to go through the eye of a needle than for a rich man to enter the kingdom of God." And they were exceedingly astonished, and said to him, "Then who can be saved?" Jesus looked at them and said, "With men it is impossible, but not with God; for all things are possible with God."

Peter began to say to him, "Lo, we have left everything and followed you." Jesus said, "Truly, I say to you, there is no one who has left house or brothers or sisters or mother or father or children or lands, for my sake and for the gospel, who will not receive a hundredfold now in this time, houses and brothers and sisters and mothers and children and lands, with persecutions, and in the age to come eternal life. But many that are first will be last, and the last first."

* * *

The wedding reception was also beautiful. The bride and groom were splendid and desirous of making a festive celebration. The grace was truly abundant. To see them there was to witness just a taste of the conquest of the treasure.

Chiara used to often say to us: "If they had only not gone away so soon." She was lamenting with a smile that the invited guests left the restaurant much before the bridal couple had hoped. They wished to stay longer and celebrate.

6

The Grace to Live Grace

Truly, truly, I say to you, you will weep and lament,
but the world will rejoice; you will be sorrowful,
but your sorrow will turn into joy.

—John 16:20

On April 14, Wednesday of Holy Week, the results of the liver biopsy arrived. It was the last exam, the one that gave the definitive sentence. Chiara was in her room with Enrico when their friend Veronica arrived. Chiara greeted her with a smile, saying: "Here you are, Veronica; finally you have come! Did you bring the veil?" Veronica knew that she had arrived at a delicate moment, but she did not understand how much. After this day, she also, like the evangelical Veronica, who dried the face of Jesus during the ascent to Calvary, would always have in her heart an icon of love. "True, we are waiting for the results," Enrico said to her.

Later the nurse brought Chiara her dinner, and, with the excuse of having him sign some papers, she asked Enrico to follow her into the corridor. Chiara and Veronica remained there talking a bit. At a certain point, noticing that Enrico had not returned, Chiara said: "Come with me; let's go look for Enrico.

Those two were speaking; perhaps I might discover him fainted somewhere." Out in the corridor, however, there was no one.

The doctor had taken Enrico aside and informed him of the results of the exam. Chiara was terminally ill. What had been a suspicion was now a certainty. There was metastasis in more areas. The doctor had wished to help Enrico inform his wife, but he had tears in his eyes and his voice was too choked up to speak.

Meanwhile Chiara and Veronica had returned to the room. Just as she was seating herself, Enrico entered and, holding back tears, called his wife. Enrico accompanied her to the hospital chapel, where he told her everything without saying anything. They embraced before the Lord and repeated their marriage vows. Out of fear that the devil might tempt her, she asked specifically: "Just do not tell me how much time remains, because I wish to live in the present."

A few moments later, hand in hand, they walked again in the corridor. Enrico was shaken, but Chiara was smiling, chatting with the nurses who stopped to speak with her. She greeted everyone. It was then time to get her things and go home.

* * *

Just the previous evening, in a conversation in her room, Chiara had described her marriage for what it was, a path to Heaven. To her, a widower had every right to remarry, precisely because it would bring him to Heaven, and that is what matters.

Sometime before, she had been interested in opening a pediatric hospice to help oncological children and their families confront death. In her head there was always something for others, and in her suffering she was drawn ever closer to the ill and the needy. Sustained by grace, she was ready to go to the end.

The Grace to Live Grace

The two spouses accompanied Veronica to the exit, where, for the first time, her friend saw Chiara cry. They said good-bye in silence; then Chiara was able to say, "Well then, happy Easter."

Enrico left the hospital alone and went straight to his in-laws to tell them the news and to pick up little Francesco. When he returned, Chiara was in the chapel. Seeing Francesco, she took him in her arms and, showing him a picture of the Virgin Mary, helped him to light a candle. Chiara once again found herself before an image of the Virgin Mary, as in the beginning with Maria Grazia Letizia. If it is true that we are what we love, and Chiara loved Jesus profoundly, then precisely during these last trials, she was becoming more and more similar to her Master.

With her, everything seemed spontaneous yet precise at the same time: we found ourselves always together in the crucial moments. That afternoon when Cristiana went to see her in the hospital she did not yet know anything. Entering her room, she did not find her. They were all in the chapel: Chiara, Enrico, Francesco, Daniela, and the radiologist. Everyone was in tears except Chiara, who looked at Cristiana, smiling. "Cristiana! I knew that you would come. You always arrive at the right moment. God wishes you here each time, but how come? Did you see Veronica leaving?" Cristiana still did not understand what was happening. After speaking with Daniela a little, she took Francesco into the corridor to play in order to leave his parents alone together.

Then she went into the chapel again; she also felt the need. Enrico joined her, and they cried together. Enrico was speechless before the strength of his wife, at her reaction to the news. Cristiana told him that we would be with him, that we would not abandon him. Enrico confided that he had need of help with the concrete matters of life for Francesco: the little outfits, enrolling him in nursery school, and all the rest. He would be confronting a new daily reality alone, and it frightened him. Just living day by day made it possible to get through it; Enrico knew it. It was painful but not unendurable; he trusted in the beauty that lifts us up.

Daniela asked Cristiana to keep Chiara company while she took her last antibiotic treatment before her dismissal. In this moment, so intense, Cristiana and Chiara were alone, face-to-face.

"Are you worried?"

"You know, Cri, I quit wishing to understand, otherwise I could go crazy. And I am better. Now I am at peace; now I take whatever comes. He knows what He is doing, and up to now He has never disappointed. Later, I shall understand. If it happened a month ago, I would not have held up. Now I can do it, if I look at today. Then for each day there is grace. Day by day, I have only to make space."

She added that reentering the hospital had been difficult, but now it was different. Then they spoke of that first day of recovery, of how difficult it had been for both; but it was precisely those moments that had prepared them for the news. There was no desperation now, just a mysterious joy that let her smile.

Those minutes were a time of incredible peace, burning like an oven that consumes the superfluous and leaves only the substance: it was love received and given. We are made for Heaven and also for friendship; it must not be forgotten.

"Poor Petrisco," Chiara said, using one of her husband's nicknames. "Now he has become mushy with me." She was worried about her husband. Cristiana told her that Enrico was well; she also reminded her that he too was prepared to live all this and that he had the necessary grace. Their friends would not leave him by himself.

"Thank you," Chiara said, smiling.

The Grace to Live Grace

After the results, the doctors tried to detain Chiara and Enrico for further tests, but they did not succeed. Chiara and Enrico understood that it was useless to remain in the hospital. There was no sense taking up space and time that could benefit others; time that they could spend together as a family with Francesco and with their families and friends. Nor did it make sense to take up another cycle of cures (it would have prolonged life just a few months and at the cost of much suffering). Chiara would not even think about it, and Enrico agreed. They refused the therapies and asked to sign the dismissal forms so they could leave. For Chiara, the only cures left were palliative and temporary, in order to soften the pain. Now she had to go and console her family.

Also at the hospital was their friend, Anna Chiara, Gigi's wife. She was pregnant and was in the hospital for a fetal monitoring and was waiting her turn. Since it did not seem opportune to speak of herself at that moment, Chiara, giving her [friend's] belly a pat, asked her what she had planned for the little one's future education. Anna Chiara and her husband already had three children. When Anna Chiara finished with her exam, she encountered the Petrillos in the corridor, returning from a visit to the chapel. Chiara seemed more luminous than ever; it was as if that situation had brought out all her beauty.

As always, Chiara put all the others before herself, and, knowing that her friend was pregnant, she was careful not to agitate her. They embraced and with a meaningful look said good-bye. Unexpectedly, Anna Chiara gave birth by caesarean section four hours later. This was considered a special gift. The little one was indeed premature, but the doctors had discovered a knot in the umbilical cord: if the pregnancy had advanced, the risk of the baby's suffocation would have been very high, especially with a natural birth.

While they were waiting for the dismissal papers, Cristiana accompanied Chiara to the room to gather her things, then she said good-bye to all her roommates. In order not to upset anyone, she explained nothing to anyone. Smiling, she just said: "I implore you, continue to pray as we have done these nights, and remember that we are here in order to make things better for others!" The stunned nurse, observing this, asked herself "What have they been doing at night?"

Nevertheless Chiara confided to Cristiana that saying good-bye to her roommates cost her more than anything else.

Then Chiara made the rounds of the nurses and doctors, all visibly emotionally exhausted, but stunned at her peace and her smile.

A little later, we were all together, the four of us. Simone had rushed from work, and Chiara and Enrico were happy to see him. Leaving, we held Francesco in the baby sling and carried the suitcases in hand. The Petrillos were ahead of us, holding each other tightly and with a strange joy on their faces.

When we said good-bye, Chiara embraced us warmly. We told her that we loved her very much, and she responded, "I love you—so much!" We were in tears, and when she got into their car, she would not turn to look at us. Enrico had asked us to remain in the area. That evening might have been the moment to pray.

* * *

The evening of April 4, all their friends gathered around the two of them to pray the Rosary at the house of Chiara's parents, near the Coliseum. She was happy to open the door to these friends, welcoming them even now in order to share these moments with them. When everyone arrived, the chairs were already arranged in a circle, ready for the prayer that for more than a year had accompanied their affairs.

Everything began in March 2011, when Chiara was operated on for the first time and the tumor was discovered. Thinking about a way to be close to her, to Enrico and Francesco, some friends, and their families spontaneously initiated a gathering to recite the Rosary. It was a simple and effective way of accompanying them on their journey and a true consolation. Once a week, the group met at one of their homes, and they all prayed together. Initially they asked solely for Chiara's cure, and then, with the passing of the weeks, other intentions were added.

Chiara and Enrico themselves often participated, and Chiara's prayers were always offered for very concrete intentions. She was flattered by all the love that she felt around her and her husband, and it was rare to hear her ask for something for herself. She prayed for babies, for the sick, for persons in need, for those she knew, and for those she did not.

Chiara's words are those of someone accustomed to speaking to God and to the Virgin Mary with confidence. She would give thanks, starting with little things, daily routines: an encounter, a word, a night spent serenely, the nearness of her friends. Then she asked with confidence of the One who knew how to listen. At the beginning and at the end of the prayer, she and Enrico sang with joy. That evening, the evening of April 4, Chiara sat in an armchair; the lights were low to avoid further irritation to her eye.

The next morning, Chiara called us to ask if Cristiana was able to join her at the house near the Coliseum, where they intended to remain for some time. Her sister, Elisa, had returned from Milan, where she now lived, and she wished to speak with her in peace. Therefore she needed someone to care for Francesco.

When Cristiana arrived, Chiara was asleep. She awakened gloomy and said that they hadn't slept all night. For her and Enrico, it had been a difficult night.

Everyone was sitting together on the divan, waiting for Elisa; Chiara's parents were understandably concerned about the dejection. For Chiara the sadness that surrounded her was an additional burden. She said, in fact, it made dealing with everything more difficult. She was in need of more grace to live this moment. And so they decided to go in search of it.

Chiara and Enrico had been to Medjugorje many times, each time to say thank you for a little possible step completed in peace; and this time also they would be able to return to the Gospa (the Virgin). That evening, they began the discussion: a small plane could be leased — traveling by ship in Chiara's condition was out of the question — to transport the Petrillos, including Francesco, and their families, plus Daniela and Angelo, their doctor friends. However, Chiara did not care for the plan. On this journey, she wished to include as many friends as possible.

The next day, April 6, Good Friday, the friends were gathered again around Chiara and Enrico, once more at the house of the Corbellas. Father Fabio Rosini had proposed making the Way of the Cross with them. When he arrived, he had a first-class relic of John Paul II, which he gave to Chiara. Then, all together, they prayed for her cure, using for the Way of the Cross the reflections that John Paul II had written in 1984, the year of Chiara's birth. Father Fabio also administered the oils of the sacrament of the sick to Chiara.

Chiara was serious, concentrated, and strong as she held her eyes closed. She remained close to the persons most dear to her: her husband, her parents, her sister, and their intimate friends. Enrico looked at her with an overwhelming sweetness; plainly he was more in love with her than ever. It was a very intense and beautiful moment.

Enrico was not angry with God (and neither was Chiara). From him came the peace and the support that sustained him. God, Enrico said, "is encountered in the flesh with the gaps from the nails and in a man hung on a Cross. God is the experience of an encounter with a man who is living and risen. Often we have compared suffering to a dance. It is God who invites us to dance with Him, and if you say yes, you discover that together with the pain there is also peace and joy."

In that moment, Chiara and Enrico were dancing with Jesus. They then asked God if they could live each day in the present, so as not to go crazy. If they thought about the past, the melancholy would destroy them; if they thought about the future, fear could assail them, because they did not know what would happen. "The past to mercy, the present to grace, the future to Providence," Enrico said. "Let us ask for grace.... The Lord hears this prayer, and the cross does not crush it: each morning grace permits us to carry it, to make it again to the evening. Like Peter, let us walk on the waters agitated by the wind, fixing our gaze on Jesus."

Cristiana, who continued to help them with the little one, was impressed by the way Chiara handled Francesco. She obviously took care of him but at a distance. She was preparing him for a gradual detachment. She explained to Cristiana that if [during this challenging time] she followed her instincts as a mother, attaching herself to her son up to the last available minute, she would have destroyed herself and the little one, who would suddenly have found himself without a mother.

One particular evening, Elisa and Cristiana wished to help Chiara bathe Francesco. And she, looking at them, stood firmly aside and said: "Now you must learn to do it!"

Enrico and Chiara were always close: each glance, each word and gesture had the flavor of eternity suspended in time. Chiara explained to Cristiana that what she had had to do for Francesco she had done. "Evidently later on there will be someone better than me. I have enjoyed Enrico; it displeases me so much to say good-bye to him now. I chose him, and to Enrico I promised my love for all my days. It would have pleased me to grow old with him!"

* * *

Dearest friends,

As many of you know, during Holy Week I had some tests in the hospital, and the results were not good.

The tumor for which I was operated on a year ago has spread to other parts of the body, and humanly we can do nothing more about it, except to pray and to ask God for the strength to live this trial in sanctity.

So we have decided to depart for Medjugorje, the place where God permitted Enrico and me to meet and to ask Him for His grace! Surely, we shall not return empty-handed!

If one of you decides to accompany us, not only with prayers, but also physically, we are trying to organize a flight for next Tuesday morning, April 17, and return Thursday around the dinner hour....

Time is a little tight, but having seen that many of you have expressly asked to come, we would truly like to be able to share this moment of eternity with you.

We love you all so very much,

Enrico, Chiara, and Francesco

The Grace to Live Grace

The e-mail with which Chiara and Enrico announced the trip to Medjugorje and invited friends to accompany them is a little treasure. Chiara wrote that the examinations about her health had not been good but emphasized that they were made during Holy Week, as if to say that God was watching, so He had everything under control. Therefore, clearly, if we loved her, we could not wish to divert her from that chosen path, which is the cross.

She spoke without fear of her tumor. "Humanly we can do nothing," she wrote, "except to pray and to ask God for the strength to live this trial in sanctity." Sanctity? Is there a way to live a trial in sanctity? Yes, above all with faith that God will respond, that His assistance is never lacking, that He will come and help. For Chiara, this faith was her "Here I am." She leaned on God; she believed in Him.

In the midst of so many, even the baptized, who lived as if God did not exist, once again she lived in a way that made God present. With God near her and her husband, believing in eternal life became possible for them. But this did not signify eliminating the trial; rather, it meant going through it, or above it, as Jesus on the water (John 6:16–21). "Perhaps," as Antonio Socci wrote, "true happiness lies in obeying this law."[12]

Chiara wished to bring all of us to the place where she had met Enrico, certain that she would not return empty-handed. We also were certain that we would report home with something. We thought of her cure, but we were prepared to believe that God had other plans for her. In the past, it had stumped all of us, bringing life into the heart of death. Twice, first with Maria

---

[12] Antonio Socci, *Lettera a mia figlia: Sull'amore e la vita nel tempo del dolore* (Milano: Rizzoli, 2013), 18.

Grazia Letizia, then with Davide Giovanni, a funeral was transformed into a window on eternity.

At the airport on the morning of April 17, 2012, everyone saw the bandage on Chiara's eye for the first time. She had need of it in order not to see double. For some days, she had busied herself assigning rooms for her friends, making sure that the families with children had sufficient space, and then she willingly renounced her own room for the same reason.

In the beginning, there were only a few pilgrims involved, but in the end there were 170 on the plane. Nearly three hundred had agreed to participate. Chiara had wanted everyone at Medjugorje, but she was forced to make a selection. She and Enrico decided to give precedence to the families that had to come together, without leaving anyone at home. The trip was made possible by the generosity of Chiara's family and also by the doctors, Daniela and Angelo, who permitted her to go in spite of so many doubts and preoccupations.

Chiara departed as a true pilgrim, not knowing if she would return. In the hold of the airplane there was a cylinder of oxygen, in case of necessity, but also in case, at all costs, she wished to arrive at the top of Podbrdo.

Many of the places on the plane were occupied by children of all ages. To some who asked Chiara why she was wearing a bandage, she responded that she was a masked pirate, entertaining them with a funny expression and making them laugh. It was a cheerful, festive trip; no one seemed to feel the fatigue of the journey, but one also perceived a solemn, somewhat liturgical atmosphere.

Usually a pilgrimage has a prayerful objective, but we did not know what to ask for, which miracle. We did not know the answer. We wished only to accompany Chiara and Enrico, to be with them. We only knew for certain that it was important

Chiara at age twenty, photographed at the Corbella vacation home at Pian della Carlotta.

Above: Chiara and Enrico leaving home to join the Franciscan March 2007.

Left: On vacation together at Alghero, a beach in Sardinia.

With Simone and Cristiana on their wedding day. Enrico and Chiara will marry the following month.

Outside the Church of San Pietro of Assisi, the day of their wedding.

September 22, 2008: Enrico and Chiara, the day after their wedding, at the home of Simone and Cristiana.

A closeup of Chiara taken during their honeymoon.

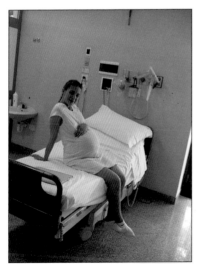

Chiara's big pregnancy with Maria, a little before her labor begins.

Enrico and Chiara with newborn Maria.

Left: Davide's secret: the Virgin Mary.

Right: Chiara greets Davide.

Below: Poster affixed to the door of the church at Davide's funeral.

l'importante
nella vita non è
fare qualcosa,
ma nascere
e lasciarsi amare

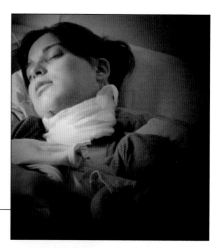

Right: Chiara after her surgery, two days after giving birth to Francesco.

Left: Enrico and Chiara walking on the bridge leaving the Fatebenefratelli Hospital. Chiara had just learned that she is a terminal patient.

Left: At the Mass at Medjugorje, Enrico and Chiara embrace after renewing their marriage vows.

Chiara on Mount Podbrdo (Apparition Hill). She, like Jesus on the way to Jerusalem, made her face hard like stone.

Chiara with her father, Roberto; her mamma, Maria Anselma; the seer Mirjana; and her sister, Elisa.

Father Vito embraces Chiara after the Mass at Medjugorje.

Chiara gives a rosary to Daniela. Chiara and Enrico's secret during times of trial: trust in the Virgin Mary.

May 2, 2012: the Petrillo family's meeting with Pope Benedict XVI.

for us to be there, to be next to them on this spiritual journey of prayer made physical in a pilgrimage.

Chiara was happy. During her testimony in the house of Mirjana (one of the seers of Medjugorje already mentioned), she told her story and that of Enrico, of their engagement and of their years as a married couple. She told of Maria Grazia Letizia, of Davide Giovanni, of the love that they had received, of the consolation that they felt, of the serenity that had been given to them.

She and Enrico returned to Medjugorje, where everything had begun, in order to know what to do, how to live this time. In each difficulty, the Father had given her a response and the strength to bear it, and she had faith that a new grace would also arrive this time.

Chiara saw with her own eyes the most beautiful miracle: the serenity in the eyes of her husband, her family, and her friends in such a difficult trial. Now, however, she wished that God would tell her if it were better for her to remain or to depart and join her other children. And if she had to depart, she added, it would be a privilege to know in advance that she was to die; thus, she would be able to say to everyone, "I love you."

For her, her husband, and all those present, she wished to ask for the grace to live grace and the gift to continue to taste hope: "I am certain that none of you will return empty-handed, because whoever receives grace will return full of grace."

When she climbed Podbrdo, "the mountain of the apparitions," that afternoon, Chiara was serene and praying. She smiled and seemed not to tire. At the peak and with a hand leaning on the railings, she knelt before the statue of the Gospa, the Virgin Mary. She asked, and she hoped. Then, with a radiant smile, she got up, and everyone prayed the Rosary together.

She, who so many times did not have enough strength to give Francesco a bottle or to hold him in her arms, had climbed all the way to the top. And once again, without the slightest hesitation, she related her story for more than an hour. Whatever the Father asked her to do; He also gave her the strength to do it. In her weakness she demonstrated grace. In spite of the fatigue and the preoccupations, also for Francesco, who was still very little, she and Enrico were living some splendid moments of peace.

Chiara was also able to meet with Ivan, the visionary of Medjugorje entrusted with praying for the sick. Chiara's mother had arranged that meeting, to which not even she knew how to present herself favorably. Her simplicity, as usual, was conquering.

"If you had the possibility of going immediately to our Lady," she asked Ivan, "would you go?"

"Yes," he responded.

"Thank you," Chiara rejoined without asking anything else. The thought that the place where Maria Grazia Letizia and Davide Giovanni are already living is a beautiful place and that they are living well was enough for her. She had nothing else to add.

On April 18, Chiara revealed the motive for her insistence on bringing so many to Medjugorje. At the end of the Mass celebrated in the chapel of the Cenacle Community, during which those present renewed their marriage vows, she and Enrico personally gave a rosary and an image of Mary to all the participants of the pilgrimage.

Smiling, they repeated Jesus' words: " 'Behold your mother' [John 19:27]. We are here in order to know their secret. This is why we wished you here, why we have brought you here—so that we may hand over to you our secret. That is, to give one another that same help that Jesus offered to the world from the Cross: His Mother, the star to follow, the one to look for in the storm."

The Grace to Live Grace

"Without Mary," Enrico told us a little earlier, "all that we were able to do would have been impossible. It was Mary who told us the truth: that there is neither past nor future; the only certainties are the present moment and the fact that we shall die. It was she, the model, who taught us to base our lives on the Word of God." It was she whom Enrico and Chiara followed.

Contrary to the predisposition to believe more easily in evil than in good, Mary bore witness to the truth that God is the good Father in whom each one can put his trust. Chiara and Enrico had done so; they accepted Mary as a Mother, they entrusted themselves to her understanding, to her love. And it worked. At Medjugorje, even they, like Mary, said to us, "Do whatever he tells you" [see John 2:5].

A sanctuary is a place that tells you: *Look at what happens to the one who entrusts himself to God; as God changes his life for him, he changes the lives of those around him.*

What Chiara did we are all called to do. We also must confront death and its hope and, in the face of fear, choose to say yes to the Father. We are all terminal patients; it is only a question of time: Chiara only preceded us, like a mother. For many it then became easier to surrender; to let themselves be loved.

Those three days—scarcely two, in reality—were, for many, a sojourn to a sacred land and that plane a type of Promised Land. On the flight, before touching ground, we became aware of what we truly were: pilgrims reaching toward Heaven. And with us, at our side, was a guide who revealed the face of God.

* * *

The month of May, Mary's month, began with the possibility of Enrico and Chiara's meeting Pope Benedict XVI. During the

Wednesday audience in St. Peter Square, May 2, they were a short distance from the parvis, the area surrounded by the colonnade. They were waiting under the hot sun until the encounter, the moment in which some of those present were able to approach the loggia (balcony) to greet the successor of Peter.

It was very hot, but when Enrico opened the umbrella to shelter his wife from the sun, a guard detached himself from the security detail to impede him. Before Enrico could explain, he heard the guard say: "To go to Paradise it is necessary to suffer."

"He does not know what he has just said," Enrico murmured to himself.

Chiara, incredibly, endured the heat with strength that at least in theory she should not have had. It was always like this, Enrico thought: she suffered, but her pains were somehow alleviated. Some were great, like the loss of vision, but they weighed so little on her with respect to how much one could have imagined. If you saw her, they seemed not to bother her at all. The Lord gave her the strength to do what she had to do. If Chiara had to meet the pope, then she would meet him, and she would have the grace to bear up for hours under a blistering sun. And that is exactly what happened.

The previous evening, after an afternoon searching in her closet for a dress that would still look good on her, Chiara could not hide her stupor about the encounter the next day: "How many graces we are receiving!" she said to Lucia.

When the moment came, Enrico and Chiara, who held Francesco in her arms, approached Benedict XVI. Just as the pope was to impart a blessing on Chiara and the little one, Enrico spoke: "Holy Father, we already have two babies in heaven."

The pope paused, looked at him, and repeated: "You already have two babies in heaven?"

But it was only a moment; protocol forbade anyone remaining in front of the pontiff for more than thirty seconds. Enrico knew it. He had been warned. He had little time to speak.

"They signal you to go away," his friend, a photographer who had helped him to be there with the pope, informed him. "Stay calm and do not look at them. If you have to say something to him, say it!"

Enrico also had to hand the pontiff an envelope. It contained their story. Enrico had summarized it the previous day in just a few lines, keeping it brief so that the pope would have time to read it, in spite of his infinite obligations. He wrote it while Chiara was ill from the effect of the morphine that she had just begun to take and that caused her much nausea. The story was brief, but everything important was there.

While Benedict XVI approached Chiara, Enrico insisted: "Holy Father, we should say that Francesco was born because Chiara postponed her treatment.... Now she is a terminal patient."

The Holy Father, thus enlightened, was moved and embraced her. As Enrico watched the pope hold her, he thought that truly they had done all that they could have done. Grateful to God, he handed him the letter and indicated to him that they were leaving. Then Enrico walked away with his wife and son.

* * *

After some attempts to remain in their own house, Enrico and Chiara decided, in the end, to move indefinitely into the Corbella family home in the Roman countryside, together with Francesco. The area, near Manziana, is called Pian della Carlotta; the house, situated at the top of a little hill, is immersed in beauty. At the bottom of the slope it opens into the Sea of Rome: the views of the sunset at the top are charming and powerful.

Chiara Corbella Petrillo

This was the refuge where Chiara spent the last month of her life. The main house was spacious, and the Petrillos, who were living in a guest house, did not have to manage everything with Francesco by themselves. They were able to be autonomous while remaining very close to the parents in case of necessity. Chiara would never return to the house where she had lived during the first three years of her marriage. [In spite of everything], it was a very beautiful period, "perhaps the only moment of my marriage where I lived a normal routine," Enrico related.

Father Vito often joined them from Cagliari (Sardinia), where in the meantime he had been transferred. On May 5, many friends were at Carlotta for a Mass together. In the Gospel of that day, Jesus said that to see the Son is to see the Father. Father Vito commented: "We, through Chiara, are seeing the Father, through her we are seeing God; this is why it is beautiful to be close to her."

During the prayers of the faithful, Chiara began to speak: "And now, Lord, I ask also for a cure, so that they do not say that I did not ask." There were some who thought that Chiara had resigned herself, that it would not please her to remain in life. It was not so. But above all, Chiara wished to do the Father's will.

As her story became known, she began to attract a continual procession of persons wishing to meet her, to know her, and to see her. "But why are they coming, and what do they intend to do here? What must I say to them? I do not have anything to say!" she declared. She was not aware of how beautiful it was to be next to her and Enrico. For some it was truly essential. Chiara was not like the majority of the terminally ill, who were grasping at life with all their forces. After having listened to or seen her, they returned home regenerated. She did not suck the life out of those who visited her; she donated it to them. Whoever thinks from a distance about his situation lives it with suffering;

whoever is close to it lives it with consolation, the fruit of a true wisdom.

The Rosary was moved to Pian della Carlotta and continued on Thursdays. Next to the families of always, the number of persons who wished to meet Chiara grew each time, and praying together revealed an optimal way of channeling and managing this growing presence. The Corbella family opened the doors of their own home, and nearly seventy persons arrived, so many that from the living room of a guest house, nicknamed the Cabana, where Enrico and Chiara lived, it was necessary to move into the larger "hobby," or recreation, room of the larger main house.

The evening began with personal intentions, prayers, and songs. Chiara was not always able to be there because of the pains; but if she did participate, she would also play the violin. She was always quiet, trusting, and joyous. Seated on the divan next to Lucia, who was pregnant with her fourth child, and her grandmother, when everyone rose to pray, she would say to her grandmother, "Nonna [Grandma], do not get up; stay seated next to me; we are justified!"

When Father Vito was there, he would have the adoration of the Sacrament and would pray before the exposition of the Most Holy One. Friends, relatives, acquaintances, but also many new acquaintances, who, in the meantime had known of Chiara and Enrico's story and were impressed by it, found themselves there from nine in the evening. And after having eaten, they would remain until late at night.

After a while, Father Vito asked and obtained permission from his superiors to remain with Enrico and Chiara for longer periods, even ten days, in order to accompany his spiritual daughter during the last phase of her earthly journey. His rapport with the Petrillos was very special: he recognized in them the Spouse that had made him and his priestly vocation prolific.

"I have lived this with Enrico and Chiara," Father Vito explained, "and little by little, as I got to know them, I fell in love with them. To see Chiara, who was being consumed by her illness— but in reality what was consuming her was her love for her son and her husband—it brought to mind my Spouse, who gave His body for love, who was consumed by love. I would say: 'Look how much they resemble You [Lord], look at how beautiful they are!'"

The rapport between Father Vito and Enrico and Chiara was the picture of a reality much greater than the tie between their vocations and the sacraments. The priest showed the spouses who God is; the spouses revealed to the priest the manner in which God loves.

For Enrico and Chiara, what mattered most was to be close to God, to live this trial with the Lord. They did not go searching for other doctors or alternative cures. They needed to feel God's presence. They asked for the Eucharist. Father Vito offered them the Mass daily, the adoration of the Blessed Sacrament, and confession. If the Spouse must come, it is necessary to prepare for His coming, each one with his cross. "To have the Lord at home," Enrico related, "was an incredible gift."

After the diagnosis of the terminal stage, fear was a strong temptation. Enrico and Chiara asked the Lord for the grace to live in the present in order not to go crazy; particularly Enrico. He did not know whether to say it was more difficult to be on the cross or under it, like the Virgin Mary with her Son. He loved his wife so much that he could have taken her place.

For him Chiara's tumor was like the third question Jesus asked Peter after the Resurrection. Having accompanied Maria Grazia Letizia and Davide Giovanni to Heaven, Enrico heard himself being asked once again: "Do you love me more than these?" But his answer, once again, was the same: "I understand Peter, who responded: 'Lord you know that I love you,'" Enrico said, "in the sense that You can ask me as many times as You like; by now I am in love. You know that I love You. By now 'You got me'; by now I have known You."

When there is this communion, which is not at all submission, then God can do great things. After Peter responded with his heart to the third question, Jesus entrusted to him the mission of confirming his brothers in the faith. [But first] Peter had to be aware of how much he loved his Lord. [See John 21:15–19.]

Another biblical personality offers the same reflection: Abraham had to sacrifice his firstborn, Isaac. "God knows very well that on the mountain, Abraham would have killed his son. God knows that Abraham loves Him more than he loves his son. It was Abraham who did not know it. While making that trip up to Mount Moriah, he was asking himself what could possibly happen once he arrived. Some commentators emphasize that from the verses it is not clear if God would have given Abraham another son after he sacrificed this one or if He would have stopped him before he killed him. Perhaps Abraham would have truly killed his son and then God would have raised him up. The fact is that Abraham would have had to discover that in him there was an intimacy with God more profound than anything that he had ever thought," Enrico reflected.

Enrico, also, as we have seen, after the deaths of his two children and with the illness of his wife, was having the same experience. And, obviously, so was Chiara. She also discovered how to love God above every other thing. An episode serves to illustrate it. After Chiara left the hospital for the last time, she spent that first night at home crying in anguish at the thought of how her son and her husband would be able to get along without her. It was her Gethsemane. Like Jesus, in order to go forward, she could only place her will in the hands of the Father.

The following day, she asked her husband a question. "Enrico, if you knew that your life could save ten persons, would you sacrifice yourself for them?"

Enrico responded, "Yes, if God gave me the grace."

At this point, Chiara said, "Well, even if I ask Him for a cure —and I am asking Him—perhaps God knows what I truly want." Chiara was like the man born blind, God's work was appearing in her (see John 9:1–38).

"With these words," Enrico explained, "Chiara was revealing to me that there was within her an intimacy of which she herself was not aware; that intimacy was the place where God dwells. The heart is a land we do not know well; neither its boundaries and frontiers, nor its miseries and grandeurs. In her profundity, nights and dawns were alternating, and we could discover some places only at the right moment."

Chiara related to the Father exactly like a daughter toward her own papà. One evening, May 24, during the praying of the Rosary, she spoke publicly about her fears. After the exposition of the Most Holy One, at the moment for the intentions, Father Vito invited those present to offer a prayer for healing. Chiara began to speak. She asked Jesus to cure her from the fear of wasting the seconds of her life, of not having sufficient time to complete His will; and finally she prayed that He would take from her the fear of saying stupid things, of not knowing how to respond to questions that were addressed to her. As she grew weaker, more tired, and exhausted by short breaths, Chiara revealed all her humility.

On May 30, Francesco was one year old, and the next day his birthday was celebrated in the house in the countryside.

The Grace to Live Grace

It was preceded by the Rosary, the last one in which Chiara participated. During the successive Rosaries, she remained in the guest house, watched over by Enrico and her mother, Maria Anselma.

The last days were very intense. Enrico continued to ask for the grace to live in the present, to remain under the cross next to his wife. Each morning, together with her, he placed the future in the hands of God, in order to allow them still to marvel: one step at a time, one day at a time.

After the diagnosis there were very many small, possible steps. At each stage, they discovered themselves more loved and thus more capable of loving. In love one cannot be mediocre, nor can one sustain love without work. The choices in the past were not enough, and it was necessary to choose again.

Ever more it seemed to Enrico that Chiara incarnated the little verse in Isaiah in which the prophet says: "make your face hard like stone" (cf. Isa. 50:7), a passage that prefigures Jesus when He heads toward Jerusalem to complete His mission.

As she approached the end of her life, Chiara had a fixed look, no longer deterred by foolishness. She was ever more determined to go to Paradise, to reach her Jesus—so much so that she seemed nonchalant about what was happening around her. She wished "to possess more fully everything in her Lord";[13] vigilantly and faithfully to follow the word of Jesus up to the last breath, with all the zeal and fervor she possessed. This being her choice, she accepted the grace of living in the present.

Suffering has an end in time. The cross is a "temporary setting," as Don Tonino Bello had written. While praying the Rosary with the group, Chiara and Enrico referred to this passage, precisely in

[13] *Fonti Francescane*, 279.

the hope of loosening the anguish in the hearts of those listening to them. Daniela, who had prepared an art board with the same expression, placed it next to the crucifix in front of Chiara and Enrico's bed, in order to give them hope, and to tell them that it would not be long.

Chiara was truly on the cross. In the month of May, her pains were like those of Calvary, and she lived them in her faith, clinging to Jesus with all her strength. Her eye pained her. Upon their return from Medjugorje, she began symptomatic radiotherapy to alleviate the suffering. The cure diminished the intensity of the pain; however, it did not eliminate or resolve the diplopia (double vision). Her mouth, by way of the metastasis on her neck, caused her terrible pain — so much so that she often had problems even opening it. She would swallow the medicines, helping herself with a wafer soaked in water. Moreover, she had severe thoracic pain, and with each cough she felt as if her upper and lower back were being pierced. Because of her tumor, the pleurae around the lungs, which usually are placed one over the other, tended to stick together and then to tear apart.

In the end, the cough was provoked by the tumor in the windpipe and when the fits of coughing came in a series, they also brought vomit. The sense of nausea was then uninterrupted because of the morphine therapy, although the doctors attempted to administer it in doses that would lessen the pain and at the same time not induce vomiting.

As if this were not enough, the breathlessness and exhaustion increased, and nearly each day a new swelling [a tumor] would appear on her body where the previous day she had felt a new pain. Chiara would say: "Look! It's the little dragon."

There was no disharmony between Chiara and her body: yes, she suffered, but her body belonged to her; therefore, she did not scorn it. For her, as it is for all those who say they follow Jesus, she existed only for the present moment. Chiara obeyed each day. There was no tomorrow or yesterday, only today. Despite her minimal strengths, she lived charity as much as possible, as when, during a Mass, she became aware that her grandmother, who had recently suffered a stroke, was experiencing a tremor to her leg, which caused her foot to move forward from her wheel-chair. No one was aware of it except Chiara, so, although in pain, she got up and put [the foot] back into its place. In the same way, she prepared a gift package for Gaia, her terminally ill friend with whom she was sharing her cross. Among the contents, the package included a monogrammed sweatshirt with a line from a popular stage play: "The night must pass (somehow)!"[14]

Love completely possessed her, in the only way that one could be completely possessed by something, in the Lord. While Chiara was being consumed, losing physical strength hour by hour, another life was shining more luminously within her. And the spirit of Chiara was ever more energized.

The heart of Enrico was also being prepared, so that he came to think: "My wife is going toward One who loves her more than I. Why should I be discontented?" Chiara asked him what would impress him more, a woman cured of a tumor or a papà happy with the baby without a mamma?

During this period, we spent much time on the phone with Enrico. Among the tears there was also incredible beauty and even some laughs. Chiara herself, for example, in relating her

[14] "Ha da passa' a nuttata" is the last phrase in a play by Eduardo de Felippo, *Napoli milonaria!* Eduardo is prepared to sit out the night with his daughter, who is ill, while the rest of the family is in chaos: "The night must pass (somehow)."

adventures with morphine, told us that she would see flamingos around her after taking the anti-pain pills.

When we returned to Rome to visit her, her movements were a little slowed from the drugs. She told us of her preoccupations for Francesco, how living with her family proved to be so practical and in certain ways easier. But in the house there had also been tensions, and there continued to be. Managing everyone during that phase was not easy: "You know how much Francesco has need of routine. Enrico is his father, and he will be the only one to decide the rhythms, as is just." She was very determined and completely lucid.

During these months, Angelo was always present. As a doctor, it was not easy to be next to an atypical patient who did not complain and did not seek attention for herself; it was difficult even to guess her threshold of pain. As he assisted her in these hours, Chiara reminded him of Uriah the Hittite, [King David's] general and the husband of Bathsheba, who remained faithful to his army even during the drunkenness [see 2 Sam. 11:13].

In the same way, Chiara held to the right track. The suffering squeezed her; it would by necessity show her for what she really was. Otherwise she would have only been able to demonstrate her desperation; instead she remained firm. Under the millstone, she gave her best. She told us that in spite of the malady, she cared about being beautiful for Enrico; she took care not to neglect her dress and appearance, and she tried to remain attractive. They were more in love than ever. Chiara told us that we were right when, before getting married, we spoke to each other of always putting the marriage first so that after that everything would proceed with order. It was precisely what they were experiencing. Those days they were living together were very beautiful. They said they felt like they were on vacation.

The Grace to Live Grace

One morning Father Vito celebrated Mass; and also present were some Franciscan nuns of Our Lady of Sorrows who, since her engagement, had remained close to Chiara. It was from their house at Assisi that she had left dressed as a bride on her wedding day. It was beautiful to be together with them again at this time.

In the sharing after the Gospel, Chiara said: "Sometimes I have to remind God that I also have some limits. But He pushes me even further. When I speak to Him like this, He tells me that according to Him I can make it. So if now I do not feel like it, I am able to wait and do it later on." It was beautiful seeing her [still] singing and playing for her Lord.

One day, while we were eating gelato, Chiara took advantage of the occasion to joke with Cristiana and to tease her a little. Cristiana was indecisive about which flavor to choose. Chiara said to her: "Do not ask so many questions; take the one that comes and be done with it. You saw something red, you thought it was strawberry, and you did not take it. If you had trusted yourself you would have found it was watermelon, the flavor you like best. It works like this: you take the one that is given to you without any explanation and then you find in your hands what pleases you most!" She never lost an opportunity to find meaning in everyday reality and to transform it.

* * *

Chiara had three fears: pain, vomiting, and purgatory. She never said: "I am going to Paradise," precisely because she feared she must first go to Purgatory. She flew high, but she was conscious of her sins and of Heaven above her.

Already in the preceding months, Chiara had begun to be uneasy about the sacrament of penance and she confided to

Cristiana that perhaps, up to then, she had not ever made a good examination of conscience. She hoped in God's mercy, but nothing guaranteed her that everything was okay. She told Cristiana that often when she went to confession, the priests would not find any sins that merited absolution, and they would send her home with a blessing. This displeased her very much. She did not agree; she thought that she was not explaining herself. Only Father Vito, she would say, knew her well and succeeded to help her make a good confession.

On June 9, during the Mass of Corpus Christi, the Gospel spoke of Jesus' instructions to the apostles on how to prepare for the Passover supper. In the guesthouse there were so many little children that there was also some obvious chaos, and Chiara found the situation a little upsetting. But during the Prayer of the Faithful, she gave thanks for all the babies present and for their voices, because, she said, they show us what we are; we are capricious when we wish to tell God what to do. Then she prayed to be able to have faith in the Lord's commands. And in following them, she was never deluded. Chiara would transform an occasion to complain into praise to the Father.

In spite of Father Vito's protests, Chiara convinced him to return that evening to Cagliari, where his brother and family were waiting for him. She told him that she would wait for him.

That evening, as it often happened, Enrico called us to speak of Chiara and of himself and how he was doing. He said that his wife was suffering and that they wished to spend a little time together with us. The following morning, June 12, we "flew" to Pian della Carlotta to see them. Chiara was again able to sit up in a chair and was happy to see us.

In those hours, however, she began to deteriorate, and her strengths were gradually leaving her.

Enrico was very beautiful during this trial. He suffered so much; feeling impotent, he said to Simone: "Love is not possession, and marriage is each one helping the other to be happy. And here we are; this is the moment, and we are here together."

Chiara asked to see Daniela. The doctor knew very well that her friend would never have troubled her for a small matter. She canceled all her appointments scheduled for that day and ran to her. After the first moment of alarm, the situation seemed to relax, but in reality it was worsening by degrees: in some moments, things came to a head, and then they would stabilize before coming to a head again.

In spite of it, the day was spent serenely; we spent hours talking. Chiara made us all laugh, perhaps like never before. The morphine made her frank. She was still Chiara, but without the filters.

We stayed for dinner with other friends. None of us knew if we should distance ourselves from one another or how much more time there was. That day we finally brought Chiara the fable for Francesco and the T-shirts with the inscription "We are born and we shall never die." We had spent many late evenings writing, designing, and checking it all from the printer. Now, after so much concern that we would not be able to finish in time, we were there with the fable and the shirts; it was the answer to a prayer.

After supper, Enrico excused himself in order to read the fable, but he was not able to; he was crying too much. He called us and asked us to read it. We gathered around Chiara's bed with Enrico. Simone articulated each word; it was like singing the Magnificat together, for all that we had shared and for all that the Lord had accomplished. We held each other tightly. Cristiana related that while we were writing it, we were so afraid of saying foolish things and transmitting them to Francesco.

Chiara told us that it was very good, and then she added other beautiful things. We shall never forget her smile in listening to all the wonders that the Lord had accomplished. She was very tired and suffered so much, but her face was disarming—an image of Paradise. She nodded with her eyes closed, remembering. Cristiana's illustrations also pleased her.

Enrico was in tears and was clinging to her. To recall all that the Lord had accomplished in her story prepared Chiara for her encounter. And then we said our good-bye to her that evening. There could not have been a better way.

So many times we said to each other that our friendship was accompanying us to the Lord in a profound and simple way. That evening brought to completion our friendship. Even though we would see each other again the day after, that was the occasion to say to each other, "I love you."

* * *

The deterioration was evident. Chiara was nearing her destination, and she asked to see Father Vito that evening. The Franciscan priest was at Cagliari for three days. Chiara asked when he would arrive; she wanted him next to her.

In spite of the difficulty tracking down a flight in such a short time, after various telephone calls and mishaps, Father Vito was able to obtain a ticket at the airport; and that afternoon he flew again to Rome. The plane landed at Ciampino Airport at 11:00 p.m.

During the trip, he asked himself if he was in effect arriving in time for Chiara's hour of transit, if she was only just waiting for his benediction.

About an hour later, he was at Pian della Carlotta, the Corbella's country home. Besides Daniela, he also found Angelo, the other doctor who in the meantime had joined the friends already gathered there. All of them had been alerted to the situation; in a few hours' time Chiara would indeed enter her agony, the throes of death.

When Father Vito went into Chiara's room, it was a powerful moment for her. Such was the effect of finding him standing before her that for a few seconds she remained stunned and mute. In the total silence, a few seconds seemed like minutes; everyone was watching. Chiara had waited for his arrival all day, and the emotion was great. At the same time, however, she had to hold back the nausea provoked by the medications and the cough. Supported by cushions while lying on the hospital bed that had arrived that same afternoon, she breathed with difficulty but sought to put into practice the procedure she was taught to stop the vomiting.

Father Vito was the only one who could chase away her morbid fear of pain, and that day he repeated it to her often, saying that it does not concern physical pain in itself, as it leads her to think. She did not wish again to doubt the goodness of the Father, she did not wish to lose her Lord again, and she did not wish to have the pain impede her from saying what she had to say.

"You see, Chiara? I have returned!" Father Vito said to her. Next to her was Enrico, who assisted at the scene with a tender look bathed with tears. Vito's soothing support comforted Chiara. He told her that she also, like Jesus on the Cross, would be able to pronounce her seven words [Father, into thy hands, I commit my spirit! — Luke 23:46]; she also will have all the breath necessary to say what she must say in order to bring to fulfillment her mission. She also would be able to say, "I love you," to her dear ones. Chiara would find the word, he joked. Always measured and controlled in her emotions, she would now say everything that she had to say. She expressed her affection for the persons who were next to her with words and hugs. She thanked everyone for their role in this story. It was late and she was very tired, but Father Vito, precisely on his own initiative, prepared everything necessary for the Mass.

Enrico would say that it was worth living his entire life solely for this Mass: "To see Chiara so in love with God was marvelous." The Mass was celebrated in the room where she slept, a small room that was transformed into an improvised and splendid chapel.

In that nocturnal liturgy, the prayer was heard that Chiara had addressed to the Father on April 4, just two months before. When they told her that the medicine could do nothing more for her, she returned home, together with her husband, and while he held her, she saw the sorrowful and disheartening expressions on the face of the one who loved her. Like this, however, she would not make it. She then asked God to change her suffering into a dance.

On June 12, in an atmosphere of grief and joy together, the persons next to her demonstrated, effectively, the grace that had transformed their funereal faces into luminous faces of emotion.

Chiara was happy, beautiful, and radiant. She spoke and laughed with those present in an atmosphere of extraordinary serenity. The Gospel was from Matthew, the episode in which Jesus said to His disciples: "You are the salt of the earth. . . . You are the light of the world" (Matt. 5:13–16). Chiara was very ill, but her face said that the pain was again "relieved," as if Someone were carrying the weight of it together with her. She was attentive to each word.

The setting of the homily was a dialogue between the priest and Chiara. Father Vito asked her if this light of the world, in

order not to remain hidden, must be placed on the lampstand.
[see Matt. 5:15]. Chiara nodded.

Then he asked her: "What is Jesus' lampstand?"

And she said, "The lampstand is the Cross."

And then he asked her: "Chiara, you are luminous because you are on the lampstand with Jesus."

And she, who first perhaps was scoffing—related Father Vito—at that moment gave a marvelous smile and confirmed: "Yes, it is so!" Chiara's expression said, "I have made it!" In those hours everything was accomplished.

Chiara had participated at the most profound intimacy with the Father: she became the friend of God. Through her sufferings she participated in the Cross of Jesus. Like Lazarus, she entered into new life (see John 11:1–44).

* * *

June 13: Chiara was dying. She spent the night speaking with her sister, Elisa, as she had only once before, the night before her wedding. During the hours they spent together, Chiara shared with Elisa her stupor and her emotion for the love that Enrico still demonstrated toward her, how he would tell her that she was beautiful, even if in that suffering she did not see it at all like this. Enrico repeated it to her continuously: "How beautiful you are, my love!"

To Elisa, Chiara said: "Do you know that Enrico truly loves me?" The look of tenderness and affection from her spouse in such a delicate situation restored in her all the love and acceptance of the Spouse who was so ardently awaiting her—that Spouse who also loved the "stigmata impressed upon her by the gift of life."[15]

---

[15] Semen, *La spiritualità coniugale secondo Giovanni Paolo II*, 58.

Chiara also had something to say to Enrico: "The thing that displeases me more than anything else is to leave you, Enrico." And perhaps this, from a mother, is difficult to understand, because [often] a mother tends to love a child more than the husband.

By then there was little time left. During the morning Chiara was attached to oxygen.

In those moments, while she was seated in the wheelchair looking lovingly toward Jesus in the tabernacle, Enrico found the courage to ask her a question that he had been holding back. He was thinking of Jesus' phrase: "My yoke is easy, and my burden is light" [Matt. 11:30]. "Chiara," he asked, "is this yoke, this cross, really sweet, as Jesus said?"

And Chiara, smiling and turning her glance from the tabernacle to her husband, said in a weak voice: "Yes, Enrico, it is very sweet." Truly Jesus had not deceived them. They were on the right course.

Enrico sent an instant message to their friends: "The lamps are lit; we are waiting for the Spouse." And a little later Roberto, Chiara's father, alerted the doctors. He was dressed in formal attire. On that very day, he was to have presented a farewell discourse to the association that he headed as president and from which he was retiring. Instead, he remained there next to his daughter.

Chiara was gasping. Enrico and Angelo lifted her up from the wheelchair and placed her on the bed, arranging it between the chair and the breathing device to which she was attached. Chiara, feeling herself being taken, began to say: "Mamma! I love you! I love you all! Papà, I love you! Elisa, I love you! I have said it, yes? I have said it! I love you all!" She repeated it also to the other friends present.

The Grace to Live Grace

In those minutes Maria Anselma approached Chiara and, turning toward the tabernacle at the foot of the bed, urged Jesus to perform a final miracle, a physical cure that she was hoping for so ardently. Chiara heard her, and smiling and moving her head, she seemed to say: "Mamma, you still have not understood!"

A little later Elisa approached her mother: "Mamma, have you not yet said good-bye? Have you not yet told her that she can go?" Chiara had waited until everyone was ready to see her depart; she waited up to the last moment. She continued to love everyone, letting herself love each one. Maria Anselma also gave in. The death throes began. Chiara would speak no more.

Chiara, on her bed, used all the forces that remained with her. Enrico, Elisa, and Maria Anselma began to sing; then they tried to pray the Rosary, but Chiara shook her head because it always tired her to use formulas.

Then Father Vito came closer to her and began to recite the Ascension Psalms (Psalms 120–134), those that the pilgrims pray when they approach Jerusalem. Listening to them now close to a dying Chiara, they were made present, revealing their true meaning. Father Vito read them one after the other, and those present can testify how Chiara's attention was captured by those words. They gave her courage.

Meanwhile, after being advised of the situation, friends and relatives arrived at Pian della Carlotta. When Chiara was sleeping, helped by the last possible dosage of medication that was given to her, she still breathed but with difficulty. One could only wait and pray. Around 11:30, her breathing changed, and she began to have pauses. Enrico was there next to her; he held her hand during these last minutes, accompanying her until the very end and whispering to her: "In peace I lie down and at once fall asleep, for it is You and none other, Yahweh, who make me rest secure" [cf. Ps. 4:8]. Then her soul dissolved like the salt that gives flavor.

Chiara died in her room at noon, freed from the fear of death. She was twenty-eight years old. She waited until everyone was ready to accept her departure, ready to let her go. In the next room, crowded with relatives and friends, everyone cried with heartfelt emotion but without desperation. Next to his wife, En-rico took up the guitar and began to play and to sing. Next to him were Chiara's parents and her sister.

Chiara was dressed in her wedding gown. Her "martyred" body was luminous and on her face she wore a smile.

Her husband wrote these words for her:

We have climbed this hill together.
We promised Him
to love each other all our days.
We waited for His coming from afar,
always with our lamps lighted, day and night.
We dreamed of seeing Him together,
but He wanted more for us.
Like the spring, He arrived in silence;
under us He made the flowers come up.
He must have accompanied us;
alone we could not have made it.
The peace of flowers was His perfume:
unforgettable
that eternity in your eyes.
I had already encountered them, but I could not
    believe it.
His eyes in your eyes and to that peace.
Only He is peace.

The Grace to Live Grace

I recognized Him from love,
so my eyes are still fixed in His,
in order not to lose you and not to fear,
and our hearts enamored on the Cross,
the marvel of spring.
What a marvel is spring!
How many times I have looked at you,
but only now has your beauty been revealed to me.
You are the most beautiful flower,
and I am the happiest bee.
I have discerned it;
He knew it always.
What a miracle life is, my love!
Always with empty hands before Him,
through all eternity always like this,
always so generous with us;
in Him is life;
in you I have experienced Him.
He chose me among thousands to accompany you;
He gave me the courage to say good-bye to you.
I thought perhaps that happiness was finished,
but then Francesco reminded me.
He is my trust in God.
He is the love that never disappoints.
He is the folly of the Cross of Love,
simply given.
He would say, "As the Father has sent me,
so I send you,"
but only now do I understand its meaning.
Only God can love like this;
by ourselves it was not possible to make it.

We are the wonder of spring,
which gives life to winter,
knowing that one will die happy,
because in dying death will be conquered.
I love you as the spring loves the winter,
with sweetness and in silence.
You have melted the snows for me,
in order to astonish even more
the incredulous when they shall see us return
once again,
but this time for ever
together.

* * *

The following days were very beautiful. Chiara's body was placed in an open casket in the large drawing room that so many times had hosted the praying of the Rosary and by now had become a chapel.

Dressed like a bride and with a rosary in her hand and a small bouquet of lavender, Chiara was at the center of all the prayers and celebrations. Her face was anointed with myrrh; its perfume welcomed everyone who entered. We felt as if we were on Mount Tabor, so near to Jesus, who was present and alive, that we did not wish to leave. We preferred to make three tents and remain [see Matt. 17:1–4].

So many people came to say good-bye to Chiara that the coming and going was continuous. Everyone, from parents to acquaintances, exchanged stories of their experiences with the Petrillos.

The funeral was celebrated on June 16 in the Church of Santa Francesca Romana. The day was the feast of the Immaculate

Heart of Mary. It was a beautiful sign for Chiara, who had a special rapport with the Virgin Mary. It was the daily consecration to her Mamma (Mary) that had purified her heart, freeing it from all that defiled it.

Concelebrating the Mass were twenty priests. The church was packed. It was an overwhelming sign, extremely sweet and unexpected. For Chiara's parents, whose home had become a mecca, it was a real consolation. Even His Eminence Cardinal Vallini, the vicar general of His Holiness for the diocese of Rome, was there. He had met Chiara and Enrico a few weeks before their audience with the pope. Also there with them was their friend Gigi, who had arranged the encounters with the cardinal and with the pope and who, in spite of his modest protests, Chiara had detained in order to thank him. That day the cardinal had also been very affectionate with them. His words at the funeral were beautiful. He defined Chiara as a second Gianna Beretta Molla,[16] and he said that "life is like a tapestry of which we see the reverse, the untidy part that is filled with threads. From time to time, however, faith permits us to see an edge from the smooth part." He concluded: "What God has prepared through her is something we can never lose."

Enrico was profoundly happy. It was not a joy that eliminated sorrow and tears; rather, it collected them. It was a supreme consolation to know that Chiara brought a part of him to Jesus, the Spouse of both, the one they awaited with lanterns lit, the one for love of whom they accepted ascending the cross.

---

[16] St. Gianna Beretta Molla (1922–1962) a was a pediatrician and mother who is best known for refusing an abortion and a hysterectomy when she was pregnant with her fourth child despite knowing that continuing with the pregnancy could result in her death.

"I do not think that there is a greater miracle than peace in death. For me this was the most precious pearl, the pearl worth more than all you have," said Enrico.

The altar was filled with little plants that his wife had asked him to buy. She did not want people bringing flowers to her funeral; rather, she desired that they return home with a sign that would remind them of something fundamental: that life is beyond us, and it is called Jesus.

* * *

For Francesco's first birthday, Chiara searched her mind for a gift that would last. Then the thought came to her of writing him a letter. This letter was her will and testament. Here it is:

Dearest Frankie,

Today you are one year old, and we asked ourselves what gift we could give you that would last through the years, and so we decided to write you a letter.

You were a great gift in our life because you helped us to look beyond our human limits. When the doctors wished to frighten us, your life, so fragile, gave us the strength to go forward.

For the little I have understood during these years, I can tell you only that Love is the center of our life. Because we are born from an act of love, we live in order to love and in order to be loved, and we die in order to know the true love of God. The goal of our life is to love and to be always ready to learn how to love others as only God is able to teach you. Love consumes you, but it is beautiful to die consumed precisely as a candle that goes out only after it reaches its goal.

Whatever you do will have sense only if you see it in terms of eternal life.

If you truly love, you shall be aware of it by knowing that nothing truly belongs to you because everything is a gift.

We loved your brother and sister, Maria and Davide, and we have loved you, knowing that you were not ours; that you were not for us. And so it must be with everything in life. Everything that you have does not belong to you; that is so you can make it bear fruit.

Do not ever be discouraged, my son. God does not ever take anything away from you. If He takes something from you, it is only because He wishes to give you so much more.

Thanks to Maria and Davide, we are more in love than ever with eternal life, and we have stopped being afraid of death. Therefore, God has taken from us in order to give us a bigger heart and to be opened to receiving eternity during this [earthly] life.

At Assisi, I fell in love with the joy of the consecrated brothers and sisters who were living their belief in Providence. So then I also asked the Lord for this grace of which they spoke, in order to believe in this Providence, this Father who does not let you lack anything. And then Brother Vito (Father Vito) helped us to walk believing in this promise. We married with nothing, putting God in first place and believing in the love that asked us to take this great step.

We were never disappointed; we always had a house and much more than what was ever necessary!

You are named Francis precisely because St. Francis changed our life, and we hope that he will also be an example for you. . . . It is beautiful to have some examples in life that remind you that a person can demand the maximum of happiness already here on this earth with God as a guide.

We know that you are special and that you have a great mission; the Lord has wanted you from all time, and He will show you the path to follow, if you open up your heart to Him.

Trust in Him. It is worth the pain!

Mamma Chiara and Papà Enrico

Acknowledgments

We would like to thank Enrico, little Francesco, Father Vito, the families of Chiara and Enrico, the doctors, the friends of the Rosary Group, Father Francesco, and all the persons who sustained us during the drafting of this book. We could not have written it without the fundamental contribution of their testimonies, their silences, and their prayers.

Chiara has taught us what it means to experience a holy death, and she has shown us how a child of God lives. She had always trusted, even when God's plan took her own from her, when He made her go through pain and suffering.

It would have been a mistake to say that Chiara loved the cross. She loved the Person who was on the Cross; she loved Jesus. This permitted her to love even to the end; it permitted her to be happy to be able to give life to Francesco. As Enrico has written in a poem that Chiara liked very much:

> This death
> that torments us,
> its existence
> is only a door,
> Hope.

Sophia Institute

Sophia Institute is a nonprofit institution that seeks to nurture the spiritual, moral, and cultural life of souls and to spread the Gospel of Christ in conformity with the authentic teachings of the Roman Catholic Church.

Sophia Institute Press fulfills this mission by offering translations, reprints, and new publications that afford readers a rich source of the enduring wisdom of mankind.

Sophia Institute also operates two popular online Catholic resources: CrisisMagazine.com and CatholicExchange.com.

Crisis Magazine provides insightful cultural analysis that arms readers with the arguments necessary for navigating the ideological and theological minefields of the day. *Catholic Exchange* provides world news from a Catholic perspective as well as daily devotionals and articles that will help you to grow in holiness and live a life consistent with the teachings of the Church.

In 2013, Sophia Institute launched Sophia Institute for Teachers to renew and rebuild Catholic culture through service to Catholic education. With the goal of nurturing the spiritual, moral, and cultural life of souls, and an abiding respect for the role and work of teachers, we strive to provide materials and programs that are at once enlightening to the mind and ennobling to the heart; faithful and complete, as well as useful and practical.

Sophia Institute gratefully recognizes the Solidarity Association for preserving and encouraging the growth of our apostolate over the course of many years. Without their generous and timely support, this book would not be in your hands.

www.SophiaInstitute.com
www.CatholicExchange.com
www.CrisisMagazine.com
www.SophiaInstituteforTeachers.org

Sophia Institute Press® is a registered trademark of Sophia Institute.
Sophia Institute is a tax-exempt institution as defined by the
Internal Revenue Code, Section 501(c)(3). Tax I.D. 22-2548708.